# ENDOR

A compelling and easy read! An u
how to identify common traumas and how to heal from their disabling
effects. Charles and Barbara Whitfield clearly reframe these wide-
spread problems through our creative imagination and cutting-edge
common sense to raise our Energy. — Highly recommended.

J. Douglas Bremner MD
Professor of Psychiatry at Emory University
and author of *You Can't Just Snap Out of It*

Extremely important, coming at a time when our country and
the world is at a major transition point and we need both
healing and guidance, which this book so clearly gives us. The
chapters on healing trauma are worth the price of the book
alone, plus you get a whole lot more that are guaranteed to
improve your life for the better.

Jed Diamond PhD, best-selling author of
*The Irritable Male Syndrome*:
Managing the 4 Key Causes of Depression and Aggression

A rare combination of mystical wisdom and practical guidance –
for a better relationship with our self, others and God.

Bruce Greyson MD
Professor of Psychiatry & Neurobehavioral Sciences
Division of Perceptual Studies / University of Virginia Health System

A clear, concise and enjoyable update from the Whitfields'
earlier and still classic work on how to identify and heal from the
effects of living in a difficult world. A rich and powerful book.

Pat Webbink PhD, Licensed Psychologist
Adult Adolescent and Child Counseling Associates, Bethesda, MD

*Healing the Child Within* was a favorite of mine, but Charles and Barbara Whitfield have hit an even higher level by explaining a spiritual path to harness and apply Dragon Energy in our lives. An open mind will be handsomely rewarded by this passionate collection of comparisons and contrasts in finding a way to channel God's energy into ours. This will lead to a richer understanding of our life's mission and a tighter focus on its meaning and purpose.

Darrell Hall
*Discovery House / Recovery Works*
*A trauma-based drug / alcohol recovery center*

The authors show that understanding the ancient archetype of the Dragon and what it symbolizes can open a way to extraordinary transformation and the true freedom that comes through self-knowledge, wisdom and love.

Lawrence Edwards PhD
Author and teacher

I love their clear and captivating words. A refreshing and elegant way to help us reach our full potential.

Sharon Grant
Co-author A F G E S: A Guide to Self-Awareness and Change

An imaginative archetypal journey that integrates numerous esoteric traditions.

Randy Noblitt PhD
psychologist and author

## *Other Books* by the *Authors*

### Charles L Whitfield MD
- *Healing the Child Within* 1987
- *A Gift to Myself*: Workbook for Healing the Child Within 1990
- *Co-dependence* - Healing the Human Condition 1991
- *Boundaries and Relationships* 1993
- *Memory and Abuse*: Remembering & Healing the Effects of Trauma 1995
- *Misinformation Concerning Child Sexual Abuse & Adult Survivors* 2002 with Silberg J, Fink PJ
- *The Truth about Depression*: Choices for Healing and
- *My Recovery*: A Personal Plan for Healing *both in* 2003,
- *The Truth about Mental Illness*: Choices for Healing 2004,
- *Not Crazy*: You May Not be Mentally Ill 2012
- *Wisdom to Know the Difference*: Core Issues in Relationships, Recovery and Living *2012*
- *Timeless Troubadours*: The Moody Blues Music and Message 2013
- *Choosing God*: A Bird's Eye View of *A Course in Miracles*
- *Teachers of God*: Further Reflections on *A Course in Miracles* both 2010

### Barbara H Whitfield RT
- *Full Circle*: The Near-Death Experience and Beyond 1990
- *Spiritual Awakenings*: Insights of the Near-Death Experience and Other Doorways to Our Soul 1995
- *Final Passage*: Sharing the Journey as This Life Ends 1998
- *The Power of Humility*: Choosing Peace over Conflict in Relationships 2006, with co-authors Charles, Jyoti & Russell Park
- *The Natural Soul*: Unity with the Spiritual Energy that Connects Us 2010
- *Victim to Survivor and Thriver*: Hope for Survivors of Childhood Trauma, Abuse or Neglect 2011
- *A F G E S*: A Guide to Self-Awareness & Change 2013 with Cormier S
- *The Secrets of Medicinal Marijuana* 2015

### Ciruelo Cabral
- *Luz, the Art of Ciruelo* 1997
- *The Book of the Dragon* 2000
- *Fairies and Dragons* 2008
- *Infinito Interior* 2012
- *Magic Notebook* 2015 within the line of the other two Notebooks
- Several science fiction books with George Lucas and other creatives
- Several calendars see DAC Editions

"To begin with, I would like to express my sincere thanks and deep appreciation for the opportunity to meet with you. While there are still profound differences between us, I think the very fact of my presence here today is a major breakthrough."

This cartoon reminds us of the myth and reality of why — the late middle-ages Knights existed in story and legend (1,100-1,500 AD/CE). It was for *Courtly Love*, which was a medieval European *literary idea* of love that emphasized nobility and chivalry.

We address its relationship to Dragon Energy in Chapter 17 on *The Power of Love* on page 177.

'Every Love story is beautiful, but OUR's is my favorite.'
Anonymous

→ See our **Introduction** and **Table of Contents** on p xxiii.

→ And see page 23-24 that shows the **17 *Main Characteristics*** of Dragon Energy.

# *Dragon Energy*

## *Myth* and *Reality*

**Exploring the Vibrant and Creative Energy in All Humans**

**— Self-Motivated Mind and Spirit**

**Its Dimensions, Dynamics and Healing Potential**

## Charles L Whitfield MD

## Barbara H Whitfield RT

*with*
## Ciruelo Cabral

**Art, Inspiration and Commentary**

*Muse House Press*      2019

*DRAGON ENERGY*

**MUSE HOUSE PRESS**

ISBN: 978-1-935827-30-6

Trade Paperback

Copyright © 2019 Charles L Whitfield, Barbara H Whitfield

All Rights Reserved

*Visit* us on the Internet at: www.MuseHousePress.com

Muse House Press and the MHP Logo are imprints of Muse House Press.

Cover design and Interior composition by:

Charles L Whitfield, Barbara H Whitfield, Ciruelo Cabral / Muse House Press

Up to 5% of each chapter may be reproduced as quotes provided attribution to the authors is made. Other use may be made only with prior written permission of the publisher.

Direct requests to: cbwhit@comcast.net and design@MuseHousePress.com

Printed in the United States of America

**First Printing** of **First Edition (preprint)**

# Myth and Reality

→ Is **Our** *Subtitle*

→ Here **We** *Simplify it*

The **Myth** of Dragon Energy is *about*

→ *What **we** have **created** about Dragons over time.*

The **Reality** is *about*

→ *How Dragon Energy can **involve us**, we humans.*

This is because *we* have used our *creative imagination* over thousands of years to create and develop all the Mythological descriptions, stories and details that we have collectively created about **Dragons** —

The Creature that is the most *written about*, *talked* about, *drawn*, *painted*, sculpted, and shown in *film*, *television*, and science fiction and fantasy *literature*.

Our creative imagination is a key power of our human mind.

Throughout this book we will explore and describe both the Myth and the Reality of Dragon Energy.

Go to → ***How to Read This Book*** on page **xv** to get started.

The true crisis in our world is not social, political
— or economic.

Our crisis is the crisis of *consciousness*:

an **inability to directly experience**

**our true nature**, an *in*ability to **recognize this**

**nature in everyone** and in **all things**.

From *Inner Worlds, Outer Worlds* documentary

Our True Nature = Real Self experientially connected
to God, All-That-Is, The Source, many names

# TABLE OF CONTENTS

# Foreword

## *Dragon Energy:* Myth and Reality
### Lawrence Edwards, PhD

The authors of this extraordinary book have created a portal into a profoundly meaningful archetypal realm that holds wisdom, knowledge and resources to empower you to live your life more fully and authentically while being guided by the higher consciousness innate to your true nature.

We live in a time of unprecedented change that demands that we leave behind old ways of seeing ourselves and the world, which have alienated us from our real self and from our profound connection with others and all of creation and nature. This disconnection has led us into a wasteland of materialism and meaningless consumption.

That disconnect is also apparent in the common notion that we aren't part of nature; we're above it, separate from it and we can use and abuse it with few consequences. That deluded state of disconnect and the emptiness it creates will never be reversed by filling our inner void through the endless consumption our culture may offer — on the surface — as the path to happiness. The authors demonstrate that understanding the ancient archetype of the Dragon and what it symbolizes can open a way to extraordinary transformation and the true freedom that comes through self-knowledge, wisdom and love.

We may get caught in limiting and dysfunctional patterns of thoughts, feelings and behaviors, frequently as a result of trauma, neglect or abuse. When that happens — the greater wholeness of our psyche often brings into our consciousness symbols, images, dreams, and myths that are healing and balancing. Myths point to truths that may only be expressed symbolically and metaphorically. And they can be read and fully understood only by thinking symbolically and metaphorically. Interpreting myths concretely leads to either missing the truths encoded in the symbols, thus dismissing the myth as false — or reading the symbols concretely leads to fundamentalism with all its limitations and distortions.

Fundamentalism and the concrete thinking that produces it plague all spiritual and religious traditions. To avoid these pitfalls we have to refine our abilities for symbolic thinking. Developing this critical mode of thinking and unpacking the rich meanings of the Dragon archetype with its transformative power are the invaluable gifts that Ciruelo Cabral and Charles and Barbara Whitfield offer the reader through this remarkable work.

They inform the reader by sharing their depth of knowledge and insight into the profound meaning of the Dragon archetype and the power that it holds, which in truth is innate to each one of us. As you delve into this book, you'll learn of the connection between the Dragon symbol and the ancient yogic symbol of this innate power of revelation and transformation known as *Kundalini*. You'll learn of the connection between the Dragon archetype, the snake archetype and the ancient Greek symbol of the Caduceus, heralding healing and transformation. These are just some of the wisdom treasures you will discover in this book.

Contrast the wisdom of such an archetypal and symbolic exploration of the Dragon with what the highly regarded scientific publication *Scientific American*, published in their May 10, 2019 blog titled 'Here Be Dragons' by Kelly Reidy*. They take a scientific approach, which means a rationalist materialist approach, to understanding why Dragons have been a part of our collective consciousness, if not the material world, for thousands of years. Thus they don't go into the profound symbolic meanings of Dragons, but instead cite a study that showed that primates have fears of snakes, lions and eagles (not to mention many other fears) and these may be a recipe for our early imagining of Dragons. This speaks to the absurd lengths that ordinary or concrete thinking goes to in order to explain things that are trans-rational, transpersonal and only fully understood by cultivating mythic/symbolic thinking.

As the authors point out, the Dragon archetype has positive and negative, light and dark expressions. They can symbolize avaricious greed for material possessions or soaring energies of transformation and wisdom. Decades ago Ursula Le Guin wrote in her magnificent *Earthsea Trilogy*, in the third volume, The Farthest Shore**, this dialogue between the 'Archmage Sparrowhawk,' who was familiar with the wisdom and ancient knowing of Dragons even in their dark archetype, and his young companion Prince Arren as they talked about Dragons:

> 'But the dragons,' said Arren. 'Do they not do great evil? Are they innocent?'
> 'The dragons! The dragons are avaricious, insatiable, and treacherous; without pity, without remorse. But are they evil? Who am I, to judge the acts of dragons... . They are wiser than men are. It is with them as with dreams, Arren. We men dream dreams, we work magic, we do good, we do evil. The dragons do not dream. They are dreams. They do not work magic: it is their substance, their being. They do not do; they are.'

This may be one of the greatest gifts of wisdom we can imbibe from positive Dragon Energy, how to simply be, be present, be connected to all life, and discover the fullness of being. Here we will discover our freedom from compulsively doing and consuming which threatens our health and our planet.

May you awaken to your own Dragon Energy and reclaim your diamond being from the clutches of the conditioned mind!  This is your journey, your quest!

Lawrence Edwards PhD
July 2019

Author of 2 books — *The Soul's Journey: Guidance from the Divine Within* and
*Awakening Kundalini: The Path to Radical Freedom*.

www.thesoulsjourney.com

* https://blogs.scientificamerican.com/observations/here-be-dragons/ accessed 5/11/19.
**Le Guin, Ursula — The Farthest Shore; 1972, Bantam Press, pp. 36-37.

*Footnote* I have known Barbara and Charles Whitfield for 20 years. I had known them for their prior books and articles that addressed trauma recovery, Near-Death Experiences, spirituality, and the nature of consciousness. I served with them several times on conference panels that addressed these areas of our human reality. I am now honored to meet Ciruelo whose amazing art shows us all dimensions of Dragons and their Energy.

# How to Read This Book

*way beyond*

This book is ~~not~~ about Dragons and fantasy.

It is about **practical ways to make our lives go better** by **using our mind** and **Spirit** from an **expanded perspective.**

In this new book we explore and describe in some detail several old and new ways to **get Energy** — and more of it, all of which we refer to as Dragon Energy.

Our approach goes *beyond* what we have published on healing from trauma since 1987 in *Healing the Child Within* (Child Within is our True Self), its workbook *A Gift to Myself* in 1990 and our recent practical healing-related book *Wisdom to Know the Difference*: Core Issues in 2012.

Here are 5 understandings around **trauma** and Dragon Energy that we have learned — for your consideration.

→ There are no perfect human beings.

→ There is no ultimate answer to it all.

→ We **each** have the answer **_inside_** *of us* to **_find_** for **ourself**. *No one else* has *your answer.*

→ We are each a survivor of varying kinds and amounts of trauma.

→ We are each in a state of growth, stagnation, or at times unfortunately decline.

We summarize what our **mind** consists of in the **_Introduction_** below and how to *identify* and *use* Dragon Energy by using our Real Self and our powerful creative imagination.

To do that, throughout this book we describe and elaborate on how to use our **mind's** many ***powers***. These powers include several parts of our inner life and *how to handle* our **relationships** —whether good or bad— with *people*, *places* and *things* in our outer life.

The human mind is the most creative intelligence in the universe. When we connect our mind to God/Goddess/All-That-Is, we and our Dragon Energy become even stronger.

Read the **Introduction** and the **Contents** — unless you prefer to go elsewhere. See also page 116 on *How to Boost our Dragon Energy* using the Preface, Index, and Glossary.

*Footnote* * We use the terms of *Dragon* and *Energy* separately at times and use them mostly together as Dragon Energy as a *framework* for *exploring* and *activating* our basic and advanced human psychological and spiritual *potential*.

# ON THE COVER

In this painting I attempted to portray the Dragon Energy that flows in the universe just as plasma waves do. I decided to paint a prominent and colorful Dragon because it works better for a book cover. But I could have painted it less physical as if its body was made of flames that could suddenly switch into scales.

Artists sometimes need to give a concrete shape to something that simply doesn't have that. In the last few years I have painted my Dragons more ethereal and less material, as if I were painting their spirit rather than their body. *Ciruelo*

# ACKNOWLEDGEMENTS

The authors would like to thank Lawrence Edwards PhD for writing his excellent Foreword. Dr Edwards has a vast background and knowledge in modern psychology, neuroscience, meditation and spiritual traditions.

# DEDICATION

The authors would like to **dedicate** this book to...
• All seekers of peace and joy,
• All 80,000 people who attend Dragon Con each year and find some peace and joy there and elsewhere,
• All trauma survivors who may seek a new entry into healing and its multiple dimensions,
• All who may look for a new perspective or a *reframe* of their old problems,
• To all young Dragons who may find the clear advantages of having more Dragon Energy to make their life go better, especially within their body, mind and Spirit.

Here is a conversation to consider.


*Is this real?* Harry Potter asked

*Or has it all been happening inside my head?*


*Of course it is happening in your head, Harry,* Gandalf

answered. *But why on earth should that mean that it is

not real?*


~ ~ ~


What might 'inside my head' mean?

'My head' is another term for our mind, which we

describe below on page xxviii in our Introduction and

page 63.

## *Preface* - **Why We Wrote this Book**

*Starting with* **Charles Whitfield MD** — Some readers may wonder why, because I am a physician who might focus on clinical medicine, why I may address an unusual and esoteric idea as Dragon Energy. I have written and published 15 books, most on trauma and trauma psychology (at my age 81, I still see patients regularly). Over the last 5 years I have read and studied about Dragons and about our worldwide cultures that made them — for the following 7 reasons.

1) I have attended the 31-year-old Dragon Con Sci-Fi and Fantasy conference here in Atlanta for 8 years. The last 5 years Barbara and I have come to know and learn from one of, if not *the* most published and honored artist on Dragons — Ciruelo.

2) During those 5 years I have explored two key observations on Dragons: their a) *meanings* and b) *potential* to us as humans. Foremost within all this was the question 'What makes us pick Dragons so often above the many mythical creatures and monsters that we have envisioned over the ages?'

I believe that the answer is *not* limited to their appearances as we creatives have drawn, painted, written-about and included in film and even as some metal or concrete statues worldwide.

3) I believe that it is **our projections** onto them, especially their *meanings* and *potential* for us humans. **Foremost** for me, and I believe for most of us, is 4) **their Energy that we give them**, which we describe throughout this book.

We have made and still can make any person, place or thing to be mythical. Some *become* a myth, like Santa. Through our *individual* creative imaginations and our *collective* creative imaginations, *we make them up*. Through our imaginations we assign characteristics to them. *Assign* here also means to *project*. To project means to **transfer** our ideas onto something. We project our ideas onto Dragons, ideas that *come from* somewhere *inside of us*. That place inside us is our inner life. To go within we have to use **introspection,** which is the *examination of our own* **conscious thoughts** and **feelings** and *more*.

5) **Our *inner life*** has a few important parts, and foremost there is our mind. The psychiatrist Carl Jung said 'Every science is a function of the mind, and all knowledge is rooted in it. The mind is the greatest of all cosmic wonders.'

6) We three writers understand that there is **one source** for attaining **Dragon Energy**: **Our human mind**. Of course that is *our* mind — that is inside each and every one of us. Our mind is an intelligent and multiple-understanding and multiple-acting device that helps us in countless ways we have described in our prior books. But here — to get Dragon Energy — we use our mind's **skills** of **identifying**, **learning**, **finding**, **trying** them out and taking responsibility to claim, **start** and **use** our personal Dragon Energy, which we describe throughout here.

7) **In *summary***: in this book we **update from our prior work**, **expand** and **reframe** the information we have attained about our human condition, how — over the ages — we have come to treat our self and each other and how to heal from the hurtful effects of these painful life experiences.

*Why I,* **Barbara Whitfield RT**, joyfully shared in the writing of this book: Since my near-death experience (NDE) in 1975 and my subsequent research into the aftereffects including 6 years of research at a medical school, I became aware and am still aware of energy that I didn't know about in my pre-NDE life. It has a compelling and exploratory sense that is different from the usual bioenergy that we may think of based on acupuncture and yoga. It developed over time. (I describe my NDE on pages xx and 207 and 144 about Ciruelo's *Flight Instructors* oil painting).

This energy led me to meditation and prayer, wherein I was actually knowing, listening and talking to a Higher Power. And I had believed in *nothing* spiritual before my NDE. I had no interest in meditation and prayer until then, but they calmed this spiritual interest growing in me for a while. Then I started exploring personal growth books, workshops and teachers. Meaningful coincidences (synchronicities) became an almost daily occurrence that seemed to be guiding me, and they continue.  Finally, through our friendship with Ciruelo and our yearly visits at Dragon Con I started to relate my growing curiosity to the Dragon. It is our healthy Dragon Energy that takes us by the mind, heart and spirit and urges us to grow. The more we studied the myth and reality of the Dragon worldwide, the clearer they became.

Why I **Ciruelo** became a contributor —
Barbara and Charlie had the wonderful idea of writing this book and invited me to join them during our yearly meeting at Dragon Con 2018 in Atlanta. I have written several books about the universe of Dragons and have done hundreds of paintings and drawings in my 35-years-long career as a fantasy artist specialized in Dragons.

I write my books as fantasy stories and even as poetry because that's a form that I love. In this case the practical yet analytic, well thought out and scholarly approach of Barbara and Charlie gives a special depth to our book. Their published writings have always been clear and easy to understand for all readers.

My contact with Dragons has always been through art. I see them with my eyes closed and interact with them through my imagination. It's a subtle and personal connection that is hard to analyze and impossible to prove.

But it's a rich, profound and inspirational relationship that, for me, means REAL. As an artist, for me nothing is more tangible than IMAGINATION.

# Introduction

What is Dragon Energy? Throughout this book we will **describe** its Myth and its Reality — and **how to find** it **inside** *each* of **us**.

Dragon Energy (DE) is simple and complex. That is because it is mostly *about us*. We humans have mental and emotional characteristics, traits and qualities that are simple and complex. We open this introduction with the simple ones.

### How to Find Our Own and How to Use It

While Dragons and their Energy started as a legend and myth, it becomes a **Reality** when we *find our own* DE and *live by using its Powers, Qualities and Characteristics*.

Here are our briefest and simplest observations and reflections on our relationship with the Mythical Dragon and with **our own** *Real* **Dragon Energy**.

We base these on the legends and myths from countless cultures over the ages, from psychodynamic psychology, transpersonal psychology, the study of classical mythology and more.

It is remarkable that these legends and myths

*originated spontaneously* — from **thousands of years ago** —

among countless and different cultures worldwide —

cultures that *did not know much about each other*.

**Most spoke different languages** or dialects.

Where could these myths have come from? What was their source? Wise observers called this source our **collective unconscious** mind which was described by poets, philosophers and psychologists such as Carl Jung and James Hillman.

**Notice**: *Not one* person, group, culture or country has ever *promoted* or *marketed* the Dragon as a legend or a myth. Why would we humans focus so much on Dragons unless there were one or more reasons?

**Spontaneously** here also and alternatively means that the Dragon legends and myths **came about *naturally***. They were *de novo* (Latin for 'of new' and 'from the beginning'), *unstructured*, *unplanned*, *unrehearsed* and even *instinctive*.

These characteristics support the *archetypal natures* of the Dragon that are buried *deep within our human collective unconscious* mind (see page 83 for how and why).

That spontaneous development worldwide over countless centuries and for millennia came from **one source**: our own human **creative imagination**.

Let's pause here and look at **our human condition now**.
We are not doing so well.

• Most of our life has plusses and minuses.

• No one's life is free of pain or is free from making mistakes.

• The *dark side* of Dragon Energy is ego identification and ego attachment. It can get worse when we inflate our ego with dysfunctional all-or-none thinking and behaving and more ego inflation or painful core issues.

• Please *remember*: Our ego is our false self or pretend self. How can it help us in our real life day to day?

• In tough times it may have helped us survive. But this is probably *the only way* our *ego* helps us (see charts below). Its main problem is that the ego always *has to be right and in control*. That fault causes us and others all kinds of problems in relationships when we continue to live in and from our ego.

• Living a life of repeated ego attachment makes us sick because when we are *ego attached,* our life is *out of balance*.

• Our body, mind and Spirit crave *balance* and *moderation*. Then we can move on to develop our higher needs with and through our naturally-found Dragon Energy.

• Self-learned and self-activated Dragon Energy gives us that healthy *balance* and *moderation*.

• Healing is identifying when we are **in** our ego and **letting go** of it **one day at a time**. Each time we choose to let go we will feel our burden from our past lighten up.

• We are **in our ego** when we are **not at peace** (see below).

• Once we slay our personal Dragon-ego by letting it go consistently, we can find all the dimensions of our healthy Dragon Energy.

• In this book we will identify, name and describe these dimensions and combine them with descriptions and dynamics of healthy and unhealthy Dragon Energy by one item and characteristic at a time.

## It is About Us

In the Heart of the Dragon rests its most powerful feature and strength: **Living Real**. Dragon Energy is living Real, which means living as our Real Self, our True Self, our True Identity, who we really are.

**Living Real** allows, supports and facilitates each of us to take-in a clearer picture, view and experience of reality. Living Real has a *natural boundary* built in that protects us from getting pulled back into our old unhealthy thinking and behaving patterns that may have seemed to work in the past but don't work now.

The part of us that takes in a clearer picture of reality is our powerful human mind which we describe below.

### What Living Real is *Not*

→ Living Real does **not** include habitually practicing pretending that 'all-is-well', political correctness, group think or being co-dependent — all of which come from over-attachment to our ego.

The psychiatrist Carl Jung said

*The privilege of a lifetime is **being who you are**, authentically.*

The mythologist Joseph Campbell agreed — and added —

*The goal of the hero trip* [i.e., on *our own* Hero's Journey]
*is to find those levels in the psyche* [mind, essence, soul]
*that open, open, open,*
*and finally open to the mystery*
*of your Self*
*being Buddha consciousness*
*or the Christ.*

*That's the Journey.*              from Osbon 1991 *A Joseph Campbell Companion*

Our ego's main strength is that in its limited way, it has *helped us survive*. But this is the only use of ego that we really need. In Figure I.1 below we illustrate and begin to describe how small the ego is in comparison to our mind when we are Living Real in 99% of our life as our Real Self.

**Figure I .1  Venn Diagram of Our Basic Relationship with Dragon Energy**

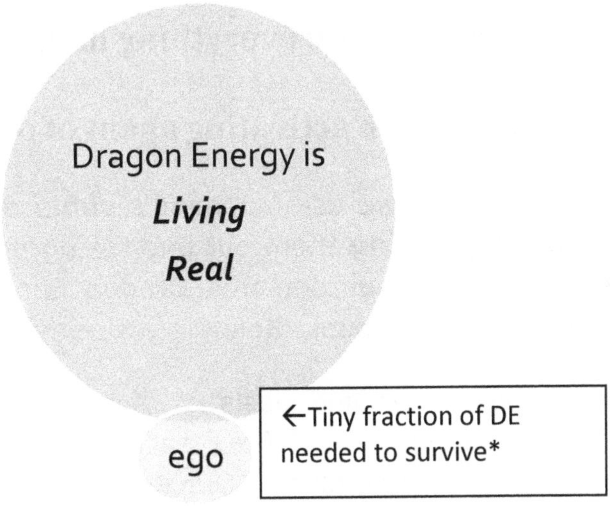

Dragon Energy is

*Living*

*Real*

ego

←Tiny fraction of DE needed to survive*

Many readers may fear or roll-their-eyes about their own potential and healthy Dragon Energy.
When we learn what DE is, we can do one simple task:
Identify when we are in our ego and let it go –
**One Day at a Time**.
* Survival is our only healthy use of ego. We can also use our *creative* and *higher* Dragon Energy to help us survive. What is most important to us is our mind, described below.

## One Source for a Good Life

We three authors know that there is **one source** through which we attain Dragon Energy and make a good life: **our human mind**. That is *our* mind — that is inside each and every one of us. Our mind is an *intelligent* and *multiple-understanding* and *multiple-acting* device that helps us in countless ways.

→ **Our mind is where everything happens.**

→ **Our mind is the activating agent of our Spirit.**

To get Dragon Energy we use our mind's **skills** of **identifying**, **learning**, **finding**, **trying** them out and taking responsibility to claim, **start** and **use** our personal Dragon Energy, which we describe throughout this book. Below is a summary (Fig I.2).

Our mind is the center and basis of our Real Self, our True Identity, who we really are. It (i.e., each of us) is in charge of making our life a success, or not. Our Real Self is the part of us that survives our body's death — which some call our Soul (pages 47ff and 63). When we live as our Real Self we can understand that we are here in a learning experience to grow psycho-spiritually exploring the Divine Mystery. Then we don't fear death the way we do when we are in our ego.

Our ego is terrified of losing control and will fight us on this idea. Once we step out of and beyond our ego, our life will be and is much easier to navigate. In our natural and healthy Dragon Energy we know this as a fact and that we are progressively ready for us to expand into living these Here and Now.

Our mind is our **one source** for attaining **Dragon Energy**

By contrast, our *ego* (our false or 'pretend' self) *acts like **it*** is God. But our ego is not real. It is not us. It is only a temporary assistant that we can call on to survive in difficult times if we know how to use it carefully.

## Figure I. 2  A Bird's-Eye View of our Mind

The **mind** is a group of mental abilities: consciousness (awareness), perception, thinking, judgement, language and memory. It has the powers of imagination, recognition, appreciation and more. It is responsible for processing feelings and emotions, resulting in attitudes and actions.

**Real Self**

Who I really am.
Who is in charge of making my life go right for *me* (but not for another person).

**Mind**

Mind is *where everything happens*

*Right* Mind is experientially connected to God.
*Wrong* mind is attached to ego.

The ego is only a helper for our Real Self. With Dragon Energy we use ego only to survive and stay safe, *not* to attack or hurt others.

**false self = ego**

Using our Dragon Energy helps us know our Right Mind if we open our conscious mind to it.

Both Real Self and ego have conscious and unconscious parts.
Until we get to know our ego, most of its actions are unconscious.

### Not the Brain

The mind is *not* the *brain*. While we are alive now our brain is an amazing organic 'hardware' that temporarily supports our mind — but cannot replace it. We can understand our mind as the ultimate, individual and sophisticated 'software.' Dragon Energy might be thought of as an 'App' that helps the hardware and software work in a more efficient way and even (if we choose) help connect us to the 'Bigger Mind' or Divine Mystery. But our mind is infinitely far greater, more powerful and meaningful than any string of algorithms anywhere. → See page 107 for a summary of the 6 names we have given to our True Identity.

# Connecting to God Makes our Dragon Energy Stronger

Our mind has a crucial part that is built-in to its spiritual 'DNA.' If we open our Real Self to adding this 'supercharger' aid we get progressively more effective Energy. This happens when we communicate, listen, feel with and talk to God through meditation and prayer or whatever spiritual practice works for us. Regular meditation and prayer give us a *direct line* to this subtle yet powerful and Intelligent Source of Energy.

This action empowers our mind. It is based on our relationship with our felt and spiritual connection to a Power and Intelligence greater than our self. Some call it God, Higher Power or Native American's Great Spirit or by another name from a longer list.

Regardless of all these names, the more we evolve as humans the closer we get to understand that there is only **One** God/Goddess/All-That-Is.

In his classic book *The Practice of the Presence of God* Brother Lawrence said "Think often on God, by day, by night, in your business and even in your diversions. He is always with you."

If referring to God as 'He' makes us uncomfortable, it is because the closer we get to the Divine Mystery the more we understand that God is before the gender split. Language is not adequate when it comes to illustrating what is beyond this physical reality. Near-Death Research consistently proves this point. Near-Death Experiencers who are interviewed all agree that language diminishes our ability to describe the beauty, wisdom and pure bliss that is ineffable.

∞ **Barbara**: For those readers who have a natural spiritual relationship with prayer, I have found that *just asking*, being as specific as possible in connecting with patience and faith to what our need is, *brings on the connection*. And believing that it is going to happen and then saying thank you when it does – gives us a stronger connection with each prayer. ∞

Teresa of Avila said that **effective prayer** includes faith, **humility**, **surrender** (let go) and a **loving attitude**.

That has worked for us consistently when we pray.

### Our ego in Perspective

By contrast, our *ego* (our false or 'pretend' self) *acts* like it is God. But our ego is *not real*. It is only a temporary assistant we can call on in difficult times. It is not us, it is not our Real Self or True Identity.

Three healers — psychiatrist Carl Jung and the great Indian teachers Muktananda and Meher Baba summarized this truth in the clearest way we have found:

### *The ego is a wonderful servant but a horrible master*.

(See Figure 1.1 above showing that *survival* is the rare choice time to use our ego)

In several of his writings, Carl Jung referred to our psychological battles with the *fiercest monsters* of them all - our egos.

Between the two of us, we have read and practiced the teachings of the modern holy book *A Course in Miracles* for 50 years (CW and BW were each prior atheists). It is the most practical and spiritually helpful and enriching holy book we have ever read. It is the most complete and sophisticated description of the ego we have found.

Among its many descriptions of ego, and its relationship to us and God, the Course says

'*You must have noticed an outstanding characteristic of every end that the ego has accepted as its own. When you have achieved it, it has not satisfied you.* This is why the ego is forced to shift ceaselessly from one goal to another, so that you will continue to hope it can yet offer you something.'
(Course reference 155T, 2:5-7)

The Course says that our *Right Mind* is when we connect our mind to God, while our *wrong mind* is our mind *attached* to our ego. Using our healthy Dragon Energy helps us experience our Right Mind if we are ready and if we open to God's loving and healing Power.

I (CW) have summarized *A Course in Miracles* in 2 short books: *Choosing God* and *Teachers of God*. The Course is also available free to read in various versions by searching on the Internet. An audio version that lasts some 23 hours read by a clear speaker is on youtube.com/watch?v=nrmFlDpeF-k

When we are aware and open to stepping outside the box of conventional ego-oriented thinking and behaving, there is nothing that can overtake our creative human mind.

The human mind is the greatest natural device and creative power in the universe — to our knowledge.

\*　　　\*　　　\*

→ Next is a **Special Section** that flowed *to* and *through* us after talking about the dimensions of Dragon Energy at last year's 2018 Dragon Con.

Our subtitle **Myth and Reality** came,

which we extended on our title page as

**Exploring the Vibrant and Creative Energy in All Humans**

**– Self-Motivated Mind and Spirit,**

**Its Dimensions, Dynamics and Healing Potential.**

→ Then throughout the fall of 2018 through 2019 we continued to correspond regularly by email, since we live in Atlanta and Ciruelo lives across the Atlantic ocean in Spain. Email us at chaswhit5@gmail.com for comments. No fire breathing please.

Here is a **Special** Book **Section**
— Beyond the usual Chapter format

*Imagine* — **FOR CURIOUS YOUNG DRAGONS**

→ Finding your Dragon Energy

See it now through a **new lens** and through a **new window** —into our potentials in healthier living.

# Know Your Dragon Energy + Activate It

**When fully developed**, Dragon Energy is a combination of **confidence**, **creativity**, **leadership**, and **more** — that most of us humans already possess, but *may not have developed*. In some people Dragon Energy gives them the ability to achieve and sometimes lead in a field — from business to art to technology to leadership and more.

Do you know any such person? Historically, among millions of examples, some observers may consider that Stephen Hawking, Martin Luther King Jr, Candace Owens, Bruce Lee, Albert Einstein, Ghandi, Nikola Tesla, Walter Russell, Michelangelo, Leonardo Da Vinci and others were gifted with this ability which in this book we call *alpha* Dragon Energy.

You can probably come up with more people who were great creators and contributors. We begin to explain these observations and summarize them below in Table S.1 The *Spectrum* of Dragon Energy in *Human Functioning* by *Levels*.

∞ *Ciruelo*: My first memory related to the Dragon Energy was when I was nine years-old and started to watch the TV series Kung Fu which became a major hit worldwide. The TV show led me to the figure of the martial art master Bruce Lee, AKA the Little Dragon, and that impressed me more since he was REAL, not a fictional character.

At that time, I started reading a weekly little magazine called Kung Fu that was written by Bruce Lee himself. In it, he would talk about ancient Chinese techniques to train body and mind in order to become an unbeatable warrior, considering one's own limits as the major enemy to defeat.

He also talked about the importance of concentration, awareness breathing, meditation and self-discipline. But above all Bruce Lee talked about the *Chi Energy*.

Learning to use that mysterious energy was the key issue in order to unchain an extraordinary power from inside which is at the same time a power present in everything. That was Dragon Energy. Bruce Lee incarnated the Dragon in all its aspects and his life inspired many generations in the past 40 years. At ten years old I started practicing Karate Do and Tae Kwon Do because of his influence, and all those teachings helped me to form my personality. ∞

[We will use this **Infinity symbol ∞** to indicate that Ciruelo or Barbara wrote the marked text. CW wrote most of the text which they *also read* and/or *edited*. We will speak at the upcoming Dragon Con in Atlanta as a panel three times in 2019.]

*Unfortunately* — for all of humankind — there were those who were destructive and had *extreme negative energy*, and did *not* have DE. Examples may come to mind — such as Hitler, Vladimir Lenin, Joseph Stalin, Pol Pot and Genghis Khan. Most of these were violent sociopaths, a toxic condition currently called *Antisocial Personality Disorder*. They and some with other personality disorders commonly **drain** our **healthy Dragon Energy**.

## *Quiet Time Works Best*

*The* **Key component** to creating and finishing jobs and projects are *long stretches* of **uninterrupted time** that give us the space and time to fully **focus** and **concentrate**. These actions raise our energy. *We are responsible to ask* for our free time.

Then, in a *positive feedback cycle* that activation for uninterrupted time *further boosts* our Dragon Energy, as in Figure X above. Many creative people and inventors have said that most of their insights and discoveries have come to them when they were **alone**.

*Example quotes:*


• **Einstein**: 'Be a loner. That gives you time to wonder, to search for the truth.'
• **Tesla**: 'The mind is sharper and keener in seclusion and uninterrupted solitude.'
• **Goethe**: 'One can be instructed in society, one is inspired only in solitude. Silence supports discovery in an open mind.'


## The *Spectrum* of Dragon Energy

Look carefully on the next page at and study Table S.1.

Notice the 4 kinds or **Levels of Dragon Energy** across the top row. Then — on the far left column — see the 15 *functions* or *features* of DE across the *spectrum* of *Dragon Energy* in levels of human functioning.

From left to right, each of these shows 4 progressively stronger increases in functioning.

Table S.1 **The *Spectrum* of Dragon Energy *in Human Functioning***

***by Levels***

| Level →  ↓Function | 4 Default | 3 Delta | 2 Beta | 1 Alpha |
|---|---|---|---|---|
| Aware | Unawareness, common | Continued decrease | Varies. Begins to decrease | Highest awareness |
| Realness | Mostly ego | Varies | | Hyper-Real |
| Decision making | Lives by ego. Traumas define choice and decisions | Varies – beginning to awaken to subtle layers | | Understands difference between ego and Real Self |
| Creative | Victim stance. | Enough | Good | Exceptional |
| Confident | Co-dependent | Varies | Present | Strong |
| Self-responsible  Self-confident | Lowest, may have an 'entitlement' mindset | Self-caring in degrees | | Highest |
| Seeks Truth | Seldom | Varies | | Most always |
| Spiritual | Varies   / Follow conventional May 'believe' but may not *Know* God | | | Knows God as a heart spirit connection |
| Co-dependent * | Most are | More | Some | Not, functions as Real Self |
| Collective consciousness from world Population | Most are asleep 'Sheeple' | Starting to awaken | Aware things are not what they seem | Collective Dragon Energy can help self & others awaken |
| Moral Compass | ego oriented | Crack in comfort zone | Begins wanting a better way | Open to my problems. Willing to help others |
| Veil Crossed into D E | None crossed | First Veil crossed | Second Veil | All three Veils crossed |
| Functioning Dimensions | 2 D Separation ~ Linear thinking | 3 D | 4 D Opening | 5 D Multi-dimensional |
| Healing from Trauma | None | Some can begin | Begins a trauma healing process | Substantial healing or low trauma history |

*Co-dependence is Focusing on others to our detriment (disadvantage, harm, impairment).
See the Glossary page 152 and my book *Co-Dependence*: Healing the Human Condition

# The Veils

Look closely below at Ciruelo's drawing of crossing the Veils into a progressively healthier function and life which will increase our Dragon Energy. This will likely happen when you cross each Veil. The drawing denotes a number of positive observations. These include:

1) The person crossing the Veils is **each** of **us** who is ultimately the Hero on our own personal Hero's Journey (see page 7 & 47).

2) The land where his feet are resting on is the 2- or 3-dimensional world of ordinary survival and ego-oriented living which has *no healthy* Dragon Energy.

3) Our Hero is kneeling on the edge of a cliff and looking out into where he can encounter the most advanced level of alpha Dragon Energy.

4) Before he can see and experience the other side as Dragon Energy, he has to *lower* his *head and shoulders* — an act which here represents humility. We define *humility* as the openness to learning more about self, others and God (in our book *The Power of Humility*).

5) But to get there our Hero will need to work through each of the 3 Veils, which we describe below.

6) The staff our Hero carries can be any or all of
• a simple walking stick,
• a tool,
• a weapon with which he can defend himself, *or*
• a *symbol* of the central Sushumna (soo/shoom/na) of the *Kundalini spiritual awakening* experience (page 98ff).

7) The **Sun** (sometimes a masculine symbol) is looking carefully at the whole scene, especially the other side of the Veil, while the

8) **Moon** (sometimes a feminine symbol) has its eyes closed — yet may be contemplating something creative and healthy.

(We remember that we each have Yin *and* Yang energy at any time whenever and wherever it will work for us).

9) The Sun ∞ Moon analogy where *opposites unite* also each reflects how by using a Tao ± Alchemy ± Kundalini approach within the Masculine-Feminine parts dwelling within each of us. 10) On the other side of the Veil, the Dragon represents our numerous potentials that can develop as we continue identifying and awakening our Dragon Energy (described throughout this book).

On the next page is Ciruelo's key creation and art drawing of

→ ***Crossing** the **Veils** into **Healthier Dragon Energy**.*

***This tells the story** of our **Journey** to **full Dragon Energy**.*

→ and **We are each the Hero**

... as we describe on **The Veils** on the previous page.

This almost 3-D drawing gives us a kind of Birds-Eye or 'Dragons-Eye' view of crossing the Veils into healthier Dragon Energy.

Now, the rest of the book awaits your **eyes**
and **mind**
and **Heart**
and **Soul**
and **Spirit**.

Who are all the ***same Being*** called ***You*** !

→ **Crossing the Veils** into a progressively healthier function and life **increases our Dragon Energy**.

Ciruelo's perfect drawing as Figure S.1 which we call the Veils follows on the next page

Crossing the Veils into Healthier Dragon Energy

**To understand the Veil,** we can each activate our own personal creative imagination (which is a key to increasing our Dragon Energy). Here 'the Veil' represents not a single Veil, but a *series* of 3 potential psychological and spiritual *healing opportunities* that we each have **surrounding** us *and* **inside** of us — **already** and **always**.

\*       \*       \*

We were inspired last year after Dragon Con 2018 when we saw a classic artwork *presented by* the astronomer and author Nicolas Camille Flammarion engraving by an *unknown artist* that dates back to 1888 in the book, 'L'atmosphère: météorologie populaire' (French for *The atmosphere: popular Meteorology*. After studying and contemplating it we conceived an expanded version which Ciruelo drew so well. (Flammarion lived for 83 years (a longer than usual life for his time) from 1842 to 1925.)

We show a copy of the original engraving on page 224 at the end of the Appendix just after the last item. The image shows a man crawling under the edge of the sky, as if it were a solid hemisphere, to look at the mysterious Empyrean beyond (a word for 'the highest Heaven' from the Greek and used later in Dante's *Divine Comedy*).

The original caption translates to 'A medieval missionary tells that he has found the point where heaven and Earth meet...' It has been used to represent a supposedly medieval cosmology, including a flat earth bounded by a solid and opaque sky, or firmament, and also as a **metaphorical** *illustration* of either the scientific or the mystical **quests for knowledge**.

We see this art and Ciruelo's perfect drawing as another of countless examples of our powerful creative imagination.

# Crossing the Veils

*Note*: This section on *Identifying* the **3 Veils** and then **working** to **cross** each Veil – slowly but *steadily* – into **activating our own Dragon Energy** → is a **simple reframe** and an **expansion** of my (CW) classic published writings on healing from mental, emotional or spiritual pain and trauma effects.

Study all of our **Know Your Dragon Energy + Activate It** section you are now reading to *Self-Empower* your **Real Self** into **healthier** and **stronger Dragon Energy.**

In my (CW) clinical work in psychotherapy with all sorts of people and most often trauma survivors — a span of from over 35 years ago — I found **4 actions** that helped us heal. These self-initiated actions involved 15 Core Issues (see page 152 for details).

To rediscover our True or Real Self and heal our Child Within (i.e., lessen our mental, emotional, physical and relationship pain), we can begin a process that involves the following four actions that include these Core Issues.

Footnote – We define the term 'Veil' as a transition point in psycho-spiritual growth, and of course not as when used in a fashion or ritual, e.g., when a bride wears a veil.

## Four — 4 — Actions to Heal

1. Discover and practice being our **Real Self** or *Child Within*. (**Being Real** is the most powerful action we can do to increase our Dragon Energy.)

> → **Key to get Dragon Energy** = Know, act and live as our **True Identity** – also called by several equally meaningful words or terms.
> These terms include: *Real Self*, *True Self*, *Child Within*, *Inner Child*, and *Divine Child*. It has also been called our *Deepest Self* and our *Inner Core*. These terms all refer to the same core part of us. One description: who we are when we feel most authentic, genuine or spirited, just to start. (I capitalize the first letters among all to show its importance for us in living and to help differentiate it from the ego, false self or lower self.)

2. Identify our ongoing physical, mental-emotional and spiritual **Needs**. Practice getting these needs met with safe and supportive people.

3. Identify, re-experience and **Grieve** the pain of our ungrieved losses or traumas in the presence of safe and supportive people.

4. Identify and work through our **Core** recovery **Issues** (listed on page 152ff).

These 4 actions are closely related, although not listed in any particular order. Working on them slowly over time, and thereby healing our hurt Real Self, generally occurs in a circular fashion, with work and discovery in one area often being a link to another area.

I describe all 4 of these actions in my original book *Healing the Child Within* and its workbook *A Gift to Myself*. Also in my recent book *Wisdom to Know the Difference*: *Core Issues* in Relationships, Recovery and Living. We summarize the details of healing in chapters 15 The Power of *Naming Traumas* and 16 The Power of *Healing from* Traumas (pages 151 and 159).

# A New Window and Lens

What is **new in this book** — from our past healing-from-trauma books — is that here we introduce *finding* and accurately *naming* the stressful and at times disabling effects of **repeated trauma** through a **new window** *and* **lens** through which some previously unknowing trauma survivors may identify. (If you happen to be one of the rare humans who have no trauma history, we may offer you some ways to help you experience more peace and joy.)

**Healthy fantasy-enjoying advantages**: For *we trauma survivors,* looking through that lens or window offers us several *advantages* — from our having an *increased imagination*, being *fantasy friendly*, having an ability to *dissociate* from physical and emotional pain, and a more *creative* mind.

## Healthy Fantasy and Dissociation Can Have — Pluses and Minuses

People who have just experienced abuse or trauma often report: "I went numb," "I just wasn't there," or "I left my body."

To *dissociate* means to *separate*. **Dissociation** is a process whereby our *experience* of something—incoming, stored or outgoing—is actively *deflected from* our *focused awareness and* our *assimilation* or *integration* with its ordinary, usual or expected mental associations.

The most common life areas here from which we can dissociate include any one or more of our senses of
•Time
•Memory
•Emotions
•Environment, our
•Identity, and our

•6 Senses (smell, touch, sight, taste, hearing and balance [from inner ear]).

We can dissociate across a spectrum of
• *healthy trance states* (from daydreaming to fantasy, role play, writing fiction, meditation and prayer)
• *defending* against *emotional* pain to
• having PTSD and/or
•a *dissociative disorder,* as shown in Figure S.2 below.

**Figure S.2. The Spectrum of Dissociation**

| | *Healthy Dissociation* | | *"Grey Zone"* | | *Unhealthy Dissociation* | |
|---|---|---|---|---|---|---|
| Healthy Trance States | Defending Against the Pain of Being Abused as a Child | | Defending Against the Pain of Being Abused as an Adult | PTSD | Dissociative Disorder | Dissociative Identity Disorder |

**Increased Creativity** ... **Survival aid** ... **Trauma Effects**

Dissociation is a *protective* and *useful* survival defense for growing up in an unhealthy family and world. When we are being mistreated, abused or neglected, dissociating allows us to separate from our awareness of our inner life, especially our painful feelings and thoughts. Here, to dissociate serves a useful purpose. It helps us get through the pain and survive.

But after we grow up and leave that unhealthy family or other difficult environment, to dissociate frequently from all pain may no longer be necessary or useful, especially if we are now around safe people. But what was an adaptive and useful skill in defending against the pain of childhood trauma may continue into adulthood as a maladaptive habit resulting in continued and increased emotional pain.

In this book — to experience our Dragon Energy and more — we are using our abilities to dissociate in **healthy** and **creative** ways by voluntarily activating our **mind's powerful creative imagination**.

∞ **Barbara**: Two of my expert colleagues — Bruce Greyson MD and Kenneth Ring PhD, both professors at the University of Connecticut — and I interviewed a base of 545 Near-Death Experiencers (NDErs) and over 1,000 more in person. One of our several important findings from our 6 years of research was that • NDErs report *childhood trauma* more often than our two other groups (those who came *close to* death with no NDE and the control group with *neither*).

The NDErs also reported that • the dissociation that they learned early-on to escape the trauma, which they now use to take their consciousness out of this reality and *move into other realms*. Ring calls that, 'A compensatory gift.' Most if not all NDErs found this to be a relief, thinking before that there was something wrong with them. In our testing, we found that most NDErs are mentally healthy in proportion to the average person and the mentally ill in our society. Our findings have been duplicated by other scientists in other parts of the world.  ∞

### Expanding the Healing Process

In the next Table we expand these above 4 classic healing actions into another dimension and realm of consciousness by humbly lowering our head and body (analogous to and from our book *The Power of Humility*) and moving through each of the 3 Veils as shown in Ciruelo's profound drawing in Figure S.1 above.

## Table S.2. Identifying the 3 Veils to Expanding Our Dragon Energy

| Veil | Actions needed to cross or Entry point into DE | Function Dimension | Comments |
|------|------------------------------------------------|--------------------|----------|
| Not one crossed | Default living; ego tends to run life | 2 to 3 D | Not knowing there are effective ways to heal, most people try to function here |
| 1st Veil | Drop our ego and be Real | 3 D | This is the *most powerful action* we can do to increase our Dragon Energy |
| 2nd | *Name* everything accurately & explore self | 4 D | This choice *avoids* the *PC trap* (*PC lowers* our *Dragon Energy*) and opens us to finding peace |
| 3rd | Connect to God experientially | 5 D | Doing this expands and strengthens our D E |

This **Special Section** you are holding in your hands now is a **creative** *expansion* of our prior **trauma, addictions** and **healing published and clinical work** for

→ **outside-the-box thinkers,**

→ **seekers of peace** and **joy,** and all people in

→ **addictions recovery** and all

→ **trauma survivors.**

This Section is also a simplified **summary** of some 30 of my (CW) works (books, chapters and peer-reviewed published articles on finding peace through and by healing from emotional pain and trauma effects.

For more details – read the 2 chapters that describe and discuss more of what we summarize here:

Chapters 14 The Power of **Naming** Traumas (p x) and
          and 15 The Power of **Healing from** Traumas (p x).

→ Man needs **difficulties**; they are **necessary for health.** *Jung*

**Naming** all these things and experiences *right*, *correctly* or *accurately* is a *key* to help us heal from our trauma effects and self-raise our Energy, which in this book we call Dragon Energy.

*Please Remember* → Living in the PC trap (political correctness compulsively) drains all our energy and it especially lowers our Dragon Energy. This is in part because *Being Real* is a primary and key characteristic of Dragon Energy.

Being Real is a healthy self-expression that helps us in **Naming** all these things and experiences. When we name them *Correctly* or *Accurately*, this is a key to 4 D living and eventually evolving into thriving in 5 D.

## Review of the Veils

### **First** Veil – **Drop our ego** and **Get Real.**

### **Second** Veil – **Name everything accurately.**
**Some key examples include:** We can name each of these below from our personal experience –

As an example → the **common string** of how most parts of our inner life **unfold** is first as our
• **beliefs**, which lead to → our
• **thoughts**, which generate → our
• **feelings**, which influence → our
• **decisions**, which lead to → our
• **choices**, then to → our
• **behaviors**, each of which are all parts of our inner and outer
• **life experiences** (from Lazaris 1988 in A *Gift to Myself*).
Naming these 6 parts of our inner life's **experiences** should also include • **any *trauma*** *influences* on each of them.

This includes our life hurts, losses and traumas, which affect each and every one of the above string. We name and discuss these in Chapters 14 and 15 (pages 149 and 157) and pages 202 and 203 in the Appendix.

When we Name everything accurately we do *not* disguise them with any *surface* names, such as 'bipolar', 'depression' or a similar label that anyone (family, friend, doctor or counselor) may have given us about our mental or emotional life. Instead – We *focus on our **real experiences*** and *process them internally* and with *safe people* who have *earned our trust*.

# No Disguise or Censorship

When we **Name** everything accurately we do *not* disguise or censor them with politically correct terms or words. *Note*: Politeness is common sense at selected times, but should not be the rule in every discussion or disagreement.

*Each of these 4 Key Actions* above (page 10) **has Energy.**
The Energy of any of our beliefs can give us only thoughts and feelings that are in harmony with our beliefs. The Energy of our beliefs, thoughts and feelings then flow and fuel on to our decisions, choices and behaviors and finally our on to life experiences.

Our hurts, losses and traumas also have Energy, but these experiences are *painful* in varying degrees. They drain our healthy Dragon Energy. But we still need to **name** them and **grieve** them in a healthy way (pages 149 and 157). What traumas we name and grieve — we do *alone* and ideally with *selected* and *trustworthy safe* and *supportive* people.
What we believe, think, feel, decide, choose and how we behave are **what we get** throughout our short life on this planet.

## Dragon Energy is *Positive* and *Optimistic*

Being *Positive* and *Optimistic are characteristics of Dragon Energy.* These are related to such psycho-spiritual skills reframing, telling our story, working any of the Twelve Steps of healing and more. Reframing is a skill of our mind to 'make lemonade out of lemons.' Healthy reframing increases Dragon Energy.

---

When we are positive any of these **6** inner life experiences — Our **beliefs, thoughts, feelings** about, **choices, decisions** and **experiences** — we will likely get positive results. These are related to the experience when we find and activate it, we get more DE. See our graphic above that these characteristics continue its Positive Feedback Cycle (Fig S.1).
By contrast, when we are negative or pessimistic, we will usually get negative results in each of these.

---

## Positive *Feedback* Cycle

A principle among the many ways we have to increase our Dragon Energy is that *each time* that we *increase* it — in a positive feedback cycle — we **get more** DE.

### Figure S.3 **Positive (+) Feedback Cycle**

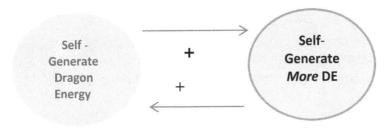

# **Third** Veil — Connect to God Experientially

Call the name for God you prefer — Higher Power, the God-of-our-Understanding, God/Goddess/All-That-Is, The One, The Almighty, Elohim or your preferred term. This **experienced connection** can include being through any or all of
• Prayer,
• Meditation,
• God-mindedness,
• God contemplation and the like.

This potentially powerful process is sacred and positive. In our and countless others' experience *prayer works best* when we have a
• Loving attitude and
• Let go and let God, i.e.,
• Turn it over, surrender, let God/Holy Spirit do its job.

∞ **Barbara:** This realm of the Third Veil is more common than we might think. NDErs, creative and/or spiritual people can enjoy this 'compensatory gift' that Greyson, Ring and I identified. That gift and ability idea started with questions about childhood trauma or childhood neglect. We found that over half (58%) of our 500 person research pool reported trauma, neglect or both. And these same people scored high on the dissociation scale. This 'ability' to dissociate and move into other realms (these 3 Veils above) is what we called a 'compensatory gift.' (Ring K *The Omega Project* 1992)

Many of our subjects relaxed when they heard our explanation because they thought there was something wrong and didn't talk about it.

What we are calling 'The Third Veil' as connecting to God here shows itself in many of our natural human traits, such as openness and gratitude, and emerges from our heart or our gut sense as joy because we can only handle so much gratitude before it pours out of us as *joy*.

I mention this several times in this book: Just as we were told by others in our culture that death is the 'Grim Reaper' (i.e., a stereotyped painful death). This is a made-up story that was created by some conventional organized religions — possibly to control us. By contrast — we (Greyson, Ring and I) showed in our research that death is a *glorious experience into the Light* (a finding that since then has been replicated by other scientists worldwide).

So too, in our Dragon Energy research we 3 authors (CC, CW and I) have had this experience as bad Dragon and good Dragon. In our vast writings on them we humans have not said that all Dragons are bad and dark. Instead, we consistently show **Dragons** as being **here to** *help us **grow*** and ***evolve***.

They are here to help us. They are the Myth/Reality that explain that this natural Energy is *in us — as us*. Just as of our own death as a trip into the Light, we believe tha Energy is already and always in us to help us grow, feel gratitude, joy, courage, and more (page 23-24 on *Characteristics*).

∞

## The Dimensions in Crossing the Veil

We source these dimensions from several psycho-spiritual thinkers and authors. We summarize what we know about them in Table S.3 below and in more detail in Appendix 9 on page 218.

### Table S.3  Dimensions in Crossing the Veil into Dragon Energy

| Dimension | Conventional Definition | Expanded Descriptions ↓ | Comments |
|---|---|---|---|
| **2 D** | width + height  (no depth) | Primitive Survival all ego | Energy limited and often low |
| **3 D =** a rare healing chance and opportunity if go into our inner life ↓ | width + height + depth (space) ... Not what we are addressing here | Ordinary Survival via ego, all-or-none / Unhealthy competition / Materialism, Energy leaks / Emptiness ... Search to fill the empty part | Unaware that our perceptions may be wrong & that we can grow. *Can heal from these trauma effects.* |
| **4 D** healing via * → the ***Portal*** | width + height + depth (space) + time (physical universe) | Let go ego / Be Real Name things accurately Explore Inner Life Learn to love self and others | Attention to •Synchronicities •Spiritual Awakenings •Trauma healing * |
| **5 D** | Transcendence via **4 D portal** to **Positive Creativity** | Connect to God experientially via meditation, prayer ... | ... words, deeds, gratitude, choose **Love over fear** |

*For Healing see Chapters 14 and 15

We each have available all of this healing from whatever inner mental and/or physical pain we may have.  We name and use the inner work we do within these increasing 3 D, 4 D and 5 D Dimensions. Doing any or all of this can be empowering as we consciously self-raise our Dragon Energy.

ᴐnsider using a geometric visual aid as a potential element into expanding our life here (Figure S.4 below). Whenever we have an issue, problem, conflict or difficulty at any time throughout our day or night, we can remember these **geometric visuals** as offering us **more** potential **paths** and **choices**.

Please study them for what each image could mean for you now and in the future.

Figure S.4 **4 + 5 D offer us More *Paths*, More *Choices* and More *Energy***

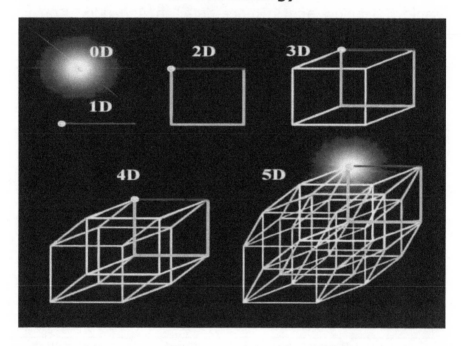

What might they offer? These images are a series of geometric metaphors for ideas to help increase our Dragon Energy via our mind's great built-in ability we have included throughout this book. This of course is our *creative imagination*. (What might the glowing light upper left signify? God's Eternal Light? Something else?)

→ Make a copy of this figure and carry it with you in case you might benefit from looking at it at some challenging time.

→ See also Table 15.1 on how to sort out the Core Issue of Difficulty Handling Conflict on page 162-165. Add it to the back of the 3-5 D visual to carry with you if possible.

## 5D Love

∞ **Barbara** We will be discussing the act of Loving several times in this book. In 3D — which is where most of us are living now, we tell someone we love what we 'Think' about their behavior or in general. This is a 3D intellectual review that may be coming from or through our 'baggage' from the past. We may not be seeing clearly yet because of the noise from our past traumas and their resulting wounds.

There is a fine line between being real and truthful to respect our own being and hurting someone we love. Many of the NDErs I interviewed and my own included report: 'Knowing the people we love, and seeing them as they will be when they grow into their full potential, gives us the opportunity to help them grow into their full potential.'

And so, instead of condemning – we separate the behavior from their being: 'You're my child and I love you! However, your behavior at this time is unacceptable. How can I help you? What do you need right now?'     ∞

For more reflections on 4D and 5D, please see the Appendix on page 218.

Our awareness of Dragon Energy ultimately comes from personal experience.

At the end of this Special Section, we *continue* from this and our above *Introduction* in Chapter 1 below.

There we describe how to *find our own* Dragon Energy and *live by using its Qualities, Characteristics and Powers.*

\* \* \*

**Yesterday I was clever,**

**so I wanted to change the world.**

**Today I am wise,**

**so I am changing myself.**

Rumi

# 1 The Power of
# Finding Our Own Dragon Energy

## *We all have Dragon Energy*

### How can we identify and activate it?

Each of us has Dragon Energy *when we*

• **learn *what it is*** and

• **learn *how*** to **activate** it. Doing so will make our life gradually work better. We will have more Energy, peace and at times joy. We do that with our usual human conflicts and down times to work through with our focused and creative mind and Dragon Energy.

Let's look at how to do these.

Here are all 17 Qualities and Characteristics of Dragon Energy (the E always capitalized and abbreviated DE):

### *Qualities* and *Characteristics* of Dragon Energy

1 - **Realness**/Being Real

2 - **Self-responsibility**/responsible

3 - **Creative**

4 - **Courageous**/Courage is to Acknowledge our fear and address what we are afraid of.

5 - **Attentive**/Attentiveness/Listen

6 - **Fully Conscious**/raised Awareness

7 - **Protective**/Protectiveness

8 - **Strong / Strength**

9 - **Optimistic** /Optimism

10 - **Positive Attitude** - becomes joyful.
Positivity makes it easier to accept joy

11 - **Zest for Life**

12 - **Sense of Humor**

13 - **Humility,** non-judgmental, non-defensive

14 - **Playful**/Playfulness

15 - **Integrity** being Real and Responsible over time

16 - **Loving**

17 - **No ego** – Let it go

Of course these DE qualities and characteristics are about us –
we humans - in our relationship with our self, others *and* how
we relate to this ages-old mythical figure.

Of these 17, we can boil them down to **7 Basic Parts –**

~ Be ~

| Real | Self-Responsible |
|------|------------------|
| Now | Non- Judgmental |
| Kind | Creative |
| Love ||

These are the 7 *basic* Qualities and Characteristics of Dragon
Energy.

## Finding Our Personal Dragon Energy

→ Dragon Energy is *our natural* Energy.
It is mostly hidden until we find it and use it for
our psycho-spiritual growth.

The **goal** is *not* to get happy and rich. The goal is to **get Real**.

Dragon Energy becomes alive for us

when we find our own Dragon Energy and live it.

Basically it's **letting go** of our **ego** and **being Real**
one day at a time.

We can personally *test* our own Dragon Energy at any instant by
*dropping* our *ego* and *living Real*.

How can we know if something is true?  The answers depend
on the human area we test, as we show in the Table.

### Table 1.1 Methods for Finding What is True

| Area Tested | Tested by | Brief Description |
|---|---|---|
| **Physical or Biological** | Scientific Method (see also Glossary on science) | Measure through our Senses ± a Control group |
| **Mind** | Observation and Interpretation | Studied by Phenomenology & Hermeneutics * |
| **Spirit** | Experience | Direct or Shared |

*Phenomenology* studies *experience* and *consciousness*.
*Hermeneutics* means *interpretation* of anything.

In summary: **Experience** happens by **Trial and Error**.

## Testing for Our DE via Scientific Method

We can **test** here by making a personal trial or self-experiment based on a theory or hypothesis that for each of us there *may be* (Myth) and *is* (Reality) such a thing as Dragon Energy.

Before we can formulate any hypothesis, we have to *imagine* that it can happen. Albert Einstein said 'Imagination is more important than knowledge. For knowledge is limited to all we now know and understand, while imagination embraces the entire world, and all there ever will be to know and understand.'

So we can first **imagine** that we have Dragon Energy. Then we formulate a *hypothesis* that **we have it**. A hypothesis (theory, premise, postulate, supposition, guess, assumption) is a *proposed* explanation for an experience or phenomenon. For a hypothesis to be scientific, the scientific method requires that we can **test** it.

The **scientific method** is an empirical (observed) step-wise way of getting information. It always involves careful observation. It includes making a
• **hypothesis** or theory based on our imagination, observations or unanswered question. Then
• **testing** what we experience and finally
• **discarding** or **refining** evidences or parts of the tested hypotheses based on our trial results. These are the 3 basic *principles* of the scientific method.
We get **empirical evidence** by *personal **observed** experience*, including *through our **senses***. Empirical further means not just observed, but first-hand, practical and experiential. Our **senses** include four areas:
• **physical** senses that include what we see, hear, touch, taste, and smell; our
• **emotional** senses span across the *spectrum* of various *emotions* that we feel; our

• **energetic** *senses* include when we feel across a **spectrum** of from low energy to motivated or invigorated *and can focus on a task*; and our

• **spiritual** senses that embody what we experience when we step outside-the-box and into the nonphysical and *transpersonal* realm.

Each of these areas includes observing and experiencing what happens in our inner life energy.

We can simplify and summarize all of this process by calling it by the *common sense* term of **trial and error**. (We can test our views and uses of anything we or others do or use — from medicines to jobs to relationships — by *trial and error*.)

### An Ongoing Process

The scientific method is an *ongoing process*. It does not deliver a simple cast-in-stone final answer. We do that by continuing to refine or expand our use of it, which we recommend as we *continue* to *develop* our *Dragon Energy* (Ongoing Process Figure 1.1 below).

In this sense our hypothesis or theory that Dragon Energy is real will be tested every time we, the individual, remembers, finds and activates our God-given and *self-activated* Dragon Energy.

# The Scientific Method as an Ongoing Process

All of this process comes from our creative imagination — which is a major strength of our mind. And our mind is likely one of the greatest developed intelligent consciousness that the Universe has ever encountered. How all this fits into the Divine Mystery of the answer to life, the Universe and everything remains a question for Dragons of all ages and degrees of creativity.

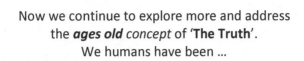

Now we continue to explore more and address
the *ages old* concept of '**The Truth**'.
We humans have been …

**Looking for the Truth** for a *Long Time*

**What is the truth?**     **Have you ever looked for it?**

→ When, where, how, for what purpose?

For your search … what happened?

We humans have searched for it for a long time.
   • How does finding 'the truth' benefit us?

      • *Where specifically* can we find it?

Let's go back a while.         Way back.

The Greek philosopher *Antisthenes*, student of Socrates, some
2,400 years ago — 400 years before Christ, warned us that

> ***The most useful*** *piece of learning for the uses of life is*
> ***to unlearn what is un***true.

→ The Greek philosopher *Phaedrus*  — 2,500 years ago
      — 500 years before Christ,
gave us a practical way to find the Truth.

> *— Things are not always what they seem;*
> *the first appearance deceives many;*
> *the intelligence of a few*
> *perceives what has been carefully hidden.*

To find the truth, the idea of **looking under** or *beneath the*
**surface** of *anything* — from rocks, to words, to stories, to

sayings, to codes — or the like — has been used for thousands of years.

It has been a foundation for the *of* ancient pro-healing, pro-growth and pro-spiritual system ~~the ancient~~ Alchemy which has been misunderstood for thousands of years. Alchemy is a *Theory* and a *Metaphor* or *Reframe* for **personal growth** by *introspection, individuation* and *balance* of the *masculine and feminine* in the Tao (page 71ff). More on it on the next page.

**Ancient Greek philosophy** arose in the 6th century BC and continued throughout the Hellenistic period and the period in which Ancient Greece was part of the Roman Empire. These Greeks used Philosophy to make sense out of the world philosophically and spiritually in a **non-religious** way. It dealt with a lot of subjects, including astronomy, mathematics, ethics, metaphysics, ontology, logic, biology, political philosophy, rhetoric and aesthetics.

> → *Phaedrus* **wasn't the only one of his time making this kind of remarkable observation.**

> → There were more creatives world-wide who said the same thing:

*Look at people, places and things* — *with a new way* or *perspective* — *beyond their surface appearance that has been carefully hidden.*

They were referring to the early church's leaders' claims that those leaders' words and practices were the only truths that we commoners should accept.
And some of us know that – that concern is still worth applying TODAY.

> → **This was the same time and era** — **about 500 BC/BCE**
> — **for several key people and events to unfold :**

**Five of the Key Events included :**
- **Ancient Greek philosophy** having started a few years earlier
- **Gautama Buddha** — Began his teachings and writings
- **Lao Tse** — wrote *The Tao Te Ching* a fundamental text for Taoism as a philosophy and spiritual way
- **Confucianism** — an early Chinese tradition, a philosophy, a religion, a humanistic or rationalistic religion, a way of governing, or simply a way of life. There was also the
- **Hebrew Bible** which came to be called *The Old Testament*. It introduced us to their positive values. See Dennis Prager's writings here.

Then Christ was born and split our record of time in half for the way we document the centuries.

Some say he was the fulfillment of the Tao. If he was the son of God, he told us, then — and so are we — each and every one of us — is a child of God when we awaken to that probability.
And if we awaken to that — we are each his brother or sister.

To help support that information, the then-early Christians developed *Gnosis* and continued through *Alchemy* — an ancient branch of Egyptian natural philosophy that existed millennia before Christ — that developed into having consistent positive associations with trade, negotiation, balance, wisdom and healing.

But over time Alchemy was misunderstood then and is still now mistaken by many due to its hidden meaning of personal growth in contrast to its on-the-surface 'turning lead into gold' which Carl Jung saw as a scientific projection. Its main pursuit was for *inner* purification and healing: Its 'gold' was the spiritual gold of the psycho-spiritual teachers, which we address also 4 pages below.

**Alchemy misunderstood** Alchemy actually meant the person making a **difficult life** into a **better life** (page 60 & 188). Today we can call it personal recovery and healing, which we describe throughout this book. See especially our Special Section on the Veils above (page 5ff) and all of chapters 14 and 15.

### Timeline of Looking for 'The Truth'

We have described a lot of useful information on finding and activating our Dragon Energy above.

We now end our description on how to address these *ages-old concepts* of The Truth with a simple Timeline in Table 1.2 below.

25,000-years-ago (i.e., 23,000 years BC) the earliest
an myth was about Ra (Re) the sun god who was said to
travelled each night through the 'underworld.' While
travelling through the underworld Ra reaches two open doors
guarded by snakes, which over the millennia and then by some
5,000-years-ago from today (i.e., 3,000 years BC) became *in
our minds* and *creative imaginations* what we know today as
Dragons.

Based on this history from anthropology, mythology and earliest
art history we can conclude and summarize that we **have
known of Dragons** for **at least 5,000 years**. *In summary*, if
we reason that our creation of Dragons has evolved from our
earliest mythological interpretation of snakes in Egypt, we can
postulate and assume that these primitive Dragons-as-snakes
existed in our *creative imagination* from at least 25,000-years-
ago. Carl Jung, James Hillman, Henry Corbin, Edward Casey and
other archetypal psychologists add that these imagined
creatures also come as Archetypes from our *collective
unconscious* mind.

Jump thousands of years to today and we find the snake/Dragon
firmly inside our past 200-*plus* years as the *Caduceus symbol*
for the professions of medicine and healing (Chapter 8, page
93). The two-snake Caduceus design has ancient and consistent
associations with trade, eloquence, negotiation, alchemy,
wisdom and healing. Today it remains as a widely recognized
symbol of healing. Most health professionals do not know that
the *Caduceus* symbol came from the *inborn*-to-us-humans and
*natural* Kundalini subtle psychological and spiritual energy,
growth and development system (pages 93, 210, 213, Table 8
A.2 on page 214 and 220).
On the bottom of the next page we show a summary in table
form of others' and our conceptions of a *Timeline* of our looking
for 'The Truth' about anything.

# Newton and James as Examples

In the 1600s, the 17$^{th}$ c. scientist **Isaac Newton** (1643 - 1726 died at age 84) liked to look everywhere for how things worked. He often *looked under* conventional scientific assumptions, which led to many of his great discoveries. This 'looking-under' to find truths was a key to his using Alchemy (the *chemistry of inner union* that used the scientific skill of 'looking under' early assumptions).

At the time Europe was dominated by the Church's power — why Alchemists such as Newton used it to survive politically. Alchemy started along with the ancient Egyptians and was carried through by the Gnostics — an early Christian group. Each group was *looking for spirituality outside the Churches' dictates*.

Moving ahead about 200 years (and 120 years ago) the pioneer physician and psychologist William James MD — who founded American psychology, said —

*The truth of an idea is not a stagnant property inherent in it.*
*Truth happens to an idea.*
*It 'becomes' true,*
*is made true by events.*
*Its 'verity' is in fact an event, a process,*
*the process namely of its verifying itself, its 'verification'.*
*Its validity is the **process** of its 'validation'.*

### Table 1.2  Timeline of Looking for 'The Truth' about Anything

| Years Ago | 300 K | 25,000 | 5,000 | 2,500 (500 BC) | 2,000 |
|---|---|---|---|---|---|
| Events | Humans begin | Egypt creates myth | Worldwide *spontaneous* creativity | * Key Events (see above) | Christ as God's son & Our Brother |
| Symbol → | Survival | Snake | Dragons | Tao | Cross |

Timeline ------ *continued*

| Years Ago | 1900 (100 AD) | 800 (1200 AD) | 600 (1400 AD) | 150 (1880 AD) | 100 (1914-18) |
|---|---|---|---|---|---|
| Events | Gnostics begin. Alchemy continues | High Middle Ages | Rennai -sance | Modern medicine begins | Trauma medicine begins * |
| Symbol → | Multiple | Creativity begins | Printing press | Caduceus with 1 or 2 Snakes on a staff | |

le **1.2** - Most Trauma medicine has addressed *physical* trauma.
**psychological trauma** has been recognized in an additional trauma
ᵣSD. *Psychological trauma* effects are **far harder to heal** (p 149 & 157).
ₙ PTSD dissociate often and have dissociation prone characteristics
for which dissociating will at times be advantageous to lessen their pain.

*           *           *

You'll find truth in your **looking glass**, not on the tongues of men.

George RR Martin

What is the **'Looking Glass'**?

The 'Looking Glass' is, with humility, going underneath the Veils

— and ***through*** them

— one by one.

***Going through the Veils*** is 'the Gold'<br>on the other side that is actually within you as you.

And find the **Hero you are** — already and always.

We believe that doing that — it takes some real and risk-taking
*curiosity* to *consider* **venturing under** the **Veils** — **1** — **by**
— **1, over as** — **long** — **a** — **time** — **as** — **it** — **takes.**

We will close this chapter with our opening → Before we can
formulate any hypothesis, we have to *imagine* that it can
happen.

Albert Einstein said -

*Imagination is more important than knowledge.*

*For knowledge is limited to all we now know and understand,*

*while imagination embraces the entire world,*

*and all there ever will be to know and understand.*

add Prager Truth = Reality
Reality is the truth maker

Of course **we humans** — in our multiple dimensions — are **still** the **biggest question and mystery** that we continue to explore in so many ways.

We are **each** individually **the Mystery**.

In our perhaps humble ***inner explorations*** we are doing that as we look at and define our human Dragon Energy.

*       *       *

In the next chapter we address *The Power of Myth*. Myth is a basic and foundational dynamic that we humans have used as we have continued to explore the Mystery of our existence and consciousness.

## Why we use 'The Power Of... '

In some Chapters we have used the terms
**The Power of** ...
to help name further qualities of Dragon Energy.

Synonyms and alternative words or terms for **Power**
include *Ability*, *Capacity*, *Potential*, *Skill*, *Strength*,
*Vigor*, *Force* and of course *Energy*.

In each of these chapters we explore and untangle more
possibilities and realities about how we can use Dragon
Energy to better our life today.

# 2   The Power of Myth

A **Myth** is a kind of cultural story that develops when enough people living in a country or region share the same narrative, legend or saga. It is their attempt to explain various parts or aspects of, what British author Douglas Adams in his 1982 best seller called, our *'Life, the Universe and Everything'* and what others and we call the *Divine Mystery*.

*Mythology* has been a serious and credible discipline within the creative arts and sciences (as Carl Jung MD, Joseph Campbell, James Hillman PhD, Grant Voth PhD and countless others over the recent centuries have described). Mythology addresses the *dimensions* of our *creative imagination.* It is a generic form of problem solving that is studied, taught and published in our universities and academic groups. It addresses how we explore, name, solve and process our *conflicts* in our personal and collective inner and outer lives. Throughout recorded history it has done so from culture to culture worldwide.

While Mythology has developed and endured as a kind of unorthodox or complimentary 'science', we are reminded of the quote by one of the world's greatest scientists Albert Einstein that 'No problem can be solved from the same level of consciousness that created it.'

In this chapter we will introduce how mythology has addressed Dragons. Later we will discuss how archetypal and self-psychology can relate to Dragon Energy.

**Our human Imagination** has been a major factor in the countless inventions and achievements that have enriched our lives. *Examples*:

• From the 1860s' first cars (called a 'horseless carriage'),
• to the Wright Brothers' 1903 invention of the first airplane,
• to computers and the Internet,
• to the great works of fiction,
    • to the imaginations of story and character in *Star Wars* and many science fiction and fantasy stories.

Myths are stories that tell us about how the collective of myth authors imagine battles between good and evil and how they see ways to handle them. Every faith and culture, both ancient and modern, has such stories. In his classic text *The Hero with a Thousand Faces* Joseph Campbell said 'Myth is the secret opening through which the inexhaustible energies of the cosmos pour into human cultural manifestation.'

Related to myth, Jungian analytic psychology has a firm effect and grasp by and among many spiritual seekers. Many of us trauma survivors are spiritual seekers, which we will develop later in this book.

One representation of the Western Dragon remains as our attachment to our ego, which is the false self. I (CW) have written and talked about our real and false self (ego) and how to use this information and heal from traumas in 15 published books and over 50 peer-reviewed published articles. And now in this book I am expanding this area which others and I call *trauma psychology* through a *new lens* — as the dimensions of Dragon Energy as Myth and Reality, with the assistance of my creative co-authors.

For over 40 years I (BW) have done extensive researcl
death and dying, Near-Death Experiences and conscious
The 'Grim Reaper' is one myth about how death greets us. we
are naturally afraid to leave our life, especially if we are still
enjoying it and don't know what could be coming next. This
myth goes far back in time and is full of fear about dying.
Perhaps paradoxically, Near-Death Experiences began as a myth
until science finally investigated these trips into the Light that
for those who are open — which has over the last 45 years has
shown us the true reality of how we die.

This is a great example of the choices we have. Do we want to
think about a nasty old bad guy with a scythe (long curved
blade) coming to get us? Or might we want to believe the
stories of now thousands of people who have died and traveled
to another reality and then come back to describe what they
experienced? When many thousands of people come back post-
NDE with the same memories can we let their stories in possibly
to open our minds, hearts and Spirits?

Indeed, from our mid age 30s we (Charles and Barbara) have
been looking at our human inner life and how, through it, we
interact with our outer life. We have written and published many
articles and books on trauma, psychodynamics and on what
psychologist Abraham Maslow called 'The Farthest Reaches of
Human Nature.' We see Dragon Energy as containing many
facets and inter-relationships among these subjects and Core
Issues in the healing process.

Addressing and understanding Dragon Energy can help us
explain these Farthest Reaches of Human Nature. This is
because our understanding of the Western Dragon has been
increasingly representing our own individual ego attachment,
which is major in our leftover issues that need to be worked
through and released. Once we 'slay our Dragon' as our
*attachment to our own ego*, we become progressively less
inhibited, more spontaneous and free to be real and identify

with the strongest features of the Western and Eastern Dragon to raise our natural communicative and Creative Energy.

In these ways and more, understanding our personal Dragon Energy helps us explore and understand our own inner life and how we interact with our outer life, which includes especially our *relationships* with people, places and things.

From early childhood most of us feared monsters and over time, as various cultures, we expanded them in various ways from gargoyles appearing in early church architecture through our art and science fiction and fantasy literature which includes popular visuals and video games as in the recently popular *Dungeons and Dragons, Magic the Gathering* and *Game of Thrones*.

## Where Did Dragons Come From?

Dragons are creatures that we humans **imagined**, **envisioned** and **created** over countless thousands of years (1 millennium = 1,OOO years). A long time ago (from as long as 25,000-years ago to as short as 5,000-years ago) enough of us became open to the idea that has developed into a kind of imaginary or fictional creature to such an extent that it has become a *living myth.* Dragons are the most *written about, talked about, drawn, painted, sculpted,* and *shown in film, television,* and *science fiction* and *fantasy literature*.

We can look at our interaction with Dragons in so many ways. Part of that interaction relates to where that living myth comes from — to **what extent we identify** with Dragons. We develop this connection in various ways throughout this book. Here is one overview of how we have viewed Dragons over these many years (table 2.1 on page 42).

After studying *World Views of Dragons* in this table, we will look at Dragon Energy as Myth and Reality. We outline these in table 2.2 on the next page. Exploring our Dragon Energy will help us *know ourselves better*. We summarize this possibility from a number of Archetypal and Mythological dimensions below.

## Table 2.1 **World Views of Dragons**

| Characteristic | Western/European | Eastern/Chinese | Other Views |
|---|---|---|---|
| **Symbolic of Functions** | **Guard, Protector** ± sometimes bad | **Transcendent, Wisdom, Good** | Independence, strength, leader |
| **Anatomic Symbols** | Has Serpent or Dragon body, *Earth* | Wings, Air, Fly, Swim | Earth v Heaven High v Low |
| **Bravery Levels** | *Protects self and vulnerable others. Fights for self-preservation.* | ***Energy of creativity*** | Fantasy creature for countless stories |
| **Below the Surface** | **We have been interested in Dragons for a way longer time than most of us can conceive. We are explaining why here.** | | No other fantasy creature has this much attention. |

## The Power of Archetype and Myth

An archetype is a universal symbolic pattern that spans a wide spectrum of experience. Archetypal characters and stories appear again and again in myths across many diverse cultures. Archetypal psychology is polytheistic in that it attempts to recognize the myriad myths and fantasies that shape and are shaped by our psychological lives. To illustrate the multiple personifications of the psyche Hillman made reference to gods, goddesses, demigods and other imaginal figures which he referred to as sounding boards 'for echoing life today or as bass chords giving resonance to the little melodies of daily life' although he said that these figures should not be used as a 'master matrix' against which we should measure today and thereby decry modern loss of richness.

Archetypal psychology is part of the Jungian psychology tradition and related to Jung's original Analytical psychology but is also a radical departure from it in some respects.

Whereas Jung's psychology focused on the Self, its dynamics and its constellations (the 4 archetypes of ego, anima, animus and shadow), Hillman's archetypal psychology relativizes and

Table 2.2 **Dragon Energy as Myth and Reality**

| Dragon Myths | | Reality |
|---|---|---|
| **Western** | **Eastern** | |
| Slay the dragon (ego) | Creative Energy | Combining Western with Eastern creates balance, flow and endless creativity |
| Joyless | Joyful | |
| Fear | Opportunity | Every fear and crisis gives us each an opportunity to learn and grow |
| Grim reaper | Trip into Light | Eastern world has less problems dealing with death |
| Courtly Love - Knights go into battle in the honor of an otherwise unreachable woman | Unconditional Love | The Energy is endless when producing love that has no traps |
| Left Brain Hemisphere | Right Brain Hemisphere | Viewed separately is incomplete. Merged, brain function is 'Holistic' |
| Yang | Yin | Opposites not only attract, they benefit one another and us |
| Individual | Group | Both important |

de-literalizes or de-mystifies the ego and focuses on *psyche*, or soul, and the deepest patterns of psychic functioning, 'the fundamental fantasies that animate all life'.

In the Eastern traditions Dragons are magical creatures with *wisdom* and *positive powers* to help us humans. Dragons in *Western* Mythology *guard* each portal/gateway to each level of Higher Consciousness.

To pass through each level we must slay our attachment to our Dragon/ego.

Dragons in *Eastern* Mythology *help us through* each portal/gateway to each level of Higher Consciousness by being the *Energy behind what we create*.

The Dragon is an **archetype within mythology**
that **describes the Energy**.
This archetype is **within us** and *all around* us
that describes part of our psycho-spiritual being.

How we relate to white doves as the Holy Spirit being in us, so
too we relate to the Dragon as part of us and collectively. We
will be describing these features throughout this book.

We use Dragon Energy to write about our experiences with our
own Dragon Energy. We are using *our* Dragon Energy as we
write our book. Now it is our job to *define* all the dimensions of
Dragon Energy.

## How Myths Work

Myths come from our imagination over time and from culture to
culture. They become accepted as universal among enough
people to call them an accepted collective story or myth.
Campbell often described mythology as having **four functions**
for us (summarized on the next page).

We keep being real and responsible for making our life go well,
which is Dragon Energy.

When we 'slay the Dragon,' one day at a time, we identify and
let go of our attachment to our personal ego.

But we will *not* profit in any way from letting go of our *healthy*
Dragon Energy. Instead, we can *learn what it is, how it works*
and *how to use it to our benefit*.

*Dragon Energy* takes the same theme and frames it through the
Heroes Journey through the power of Myth.

## Table 2. 3   The  4 Functions of Myth according to Joseph Campbell (JC) *

| Function | Comments   by Campbell and his critics |
|---|---|
| **Metaphysical**<br>Awakening a sense of awe before the mystery of being. | Mythology's first **function** is to **reunite our waking consciousness** with the **Divine Mystery**. This Mystery can't be captured directly in words or images. Symbols and myths point into the Mystery. Their enactment through ritual can give us a sense of the ultimate mystery as our inner life and our personal experiences interacting with our outer life. Metaphysics = study of being, existence, time, space, cause & more. |
| **Cosmo logical**<br>Explaining the size and shape of the universe | For pre-modern societies, myth also functioned as a *proto-science* (proto as 'first'), offering **explanations** for the **physical phenomena** that surrounded and affected our lives, such as the change of seasons and the life cycles of animals and plants. |
| **Socio logical**<br>Validate and support the existing social order | To survive, ancient societies had **to conform to an existing social order**. This is because they evolved under "pressure" from necessities much more intense than the ones encountered in our modern world. Mythology confirmed that order and enforced it by reflecting it into the stories themselves, often describing how the social order evolved from divine intervention. ** |
| **Pedagogical**<br>Guides each of us through our life stages | Myth may serve as a **guide for successful passage through the stages of one's life**. As we live we have many mental and emotional challenges. Knowing about and meditating on the universal dimensions of myths helps us navigate our life better. |

*These 4 functions appear at the end of his *The Masks of God*: Creative Mythology, and in his lectures.

** Campbell often called these 'conformity' myths as the *'Right Hand Path'* to reflect the brain's left hemisphere's abilities for logic, order and linearity.

Together with these myths however, he observed the existence of the *'Left Hand Path'*, mythic patterns like the *Hero's Journey* which are revolutionary in character in that they demand from the individual a *surpassing* of *social norms* and *morality.*

## Selected Myths Today

Over the eons we have had countless myths. Most have come and gone. Today we still have countless myths.

One big myth tries to explain how the Universe began: the *Big Bang Theory* (see Table 2.4 below). In his 2015 book *Origins: The Scientific Study of Creations*, award-winning science writer and former university professor Jim Baggott PhD (chemical physics Oxford) wrote 'Don't be fooled. No matter what you might have read in some recent popular science books, magazine articles, or news features, and no matter how convincing this might have seemed at the time, be reassured that *nobody* can tell you how the universe began. Or even if 'began' is a word that's remotely appropriate in this context.'

'If you look farther and farther away, you also look farther and farther into the past. The farthest we can see back in time is 13.8 billion years: our estimate for the age of the Universe.'

Baggott continues 'It's the extrapolation back to the earliest times that led to the idea of the Big Bang. While everything we observe is consistent with the Big Bang framework, it's *not* something that can *ever be proven*.'

But all that is based on *theoretical physics*. There *may not* have been a Big Bang that long ago. Stephen Hawking and James Hartle suggest that if we could travel backwards in time towards the beginning of the Universe, we would note that quite near what might otherwise have been the beginning, time gives way to space such that at first there is only space and no time.

Table 2.4   **Selected Myths for Consideration**

| *Myth* | *Comment* |
|---|---|
| **At *center* of every religion** | Each world religion has a birth and creation myth (e.g., Voth GL *Myth in Human History; J Hillman; J Campbell*) |
| **Big Bang Theory** | Universe's origin remains key in the Divine Mystery<br>Both a myth and science *attempt* to prove another *theory* |
| **Dragon** | The most drawn, painted, written about and wondered about non-human creature of all time |
| **Dragon Energy** | Contents of this book describe *Dragon Energy* as both a *Myth* and *Reality* in each of us wonderful humans |
| **Santa Claus** | In case a reader wonders here about good ole St Nick |

Beginnings have to do with time. This is because time did not exist before the Big Bang and the concept of a beginning of the Universe is meaningless. According to their proposal, the

Universe has no origin as we would understand it. Rather, the Universe was a singularity in both space and time, pre-Big

Bang. Thus, the *'Hartle–Hawking state'* Universe has no beginning, and it simply has no initial boundaries in time or space. Meanwhile, cute Dragons may not ponder these theories.

*      *      *

In this chapter we have described how myths are about many dimensions of our life, and how myth is related to Dragon Energy. Is there more we can say to describe how myth fits into our life?

In the next chapter we describe how our experiences today can affect our personal life and our own Dragon Energy. It may be one of the **most important and useful parts** of this book.

We call it *The Journey* Awakens the *Soul.*

# 3    The *Journey* Awakens the *Soul*

**Our Journey** is our brief life on this planet.

**Awakens** is key here, and is addressed throughout this book.

**Soul** we define first.

## *Defining* Our Soul

The 3 perennial questions remain –

1) Who am I ?
2) What am I doing here (on Earth now) ?
3) Where am I going ?

We are *each* a Soul. Our Soul is our **Real Self**.

Soul is another name or term for our Real Self or True Self or True Identity. It is who we really are in this lifetime and who we are ongoing in eternity, described below.

*One definition* of **Soul** has been that it is the
• **vital** (Energy, central, crucial),
        • **not physical** (immaterial),
        • **life principle** (life source),
generally conceived as existing within we humans and sometimes within all living things. Religion and philosophy have long been concerned with the nature of the Soul in their attempts to understand existence and the meaning of life. (from *The Columbia Encyclopedia*, 6th ed 2001-07) [our parentheses]

**Our Soul**, our true self, is the most mysterious, essential, and magical dimension of our being. In fact, it is not a separate reality, as traditional Western thought views it, but the cohesive force that unites our body, heart, and mind. It is the very *essence* of our being — author Gabrielle Roth writes

**Our Soul** always exists *for us*, *as us*, in the present moment of NOW. It does not exist in the **past** because there is *nothing in our past* that we can change. We each have our *memory* of our past experiences. Our memory *helps us learn* (if we each know how).

**Our Soul** does not exist in the **future** because the future does not exist — except in our imagination as *anticipation* or as applied *exploration*.

∞ **Barbara**: So if we are feeling bad about something in our past, or worried about something in the future – we are not in our Soul or True Self/Child Within. We are wasting time in our ego. And our ego will do everything it can to keep us in regret or worry, shame or guilt. When we are in our Soul we are here in this moment, the eternal Now. If we are here Now in the moment and we get bored, we have slipped back into our ego. To remain in the Now with our Soul/ True Self, we need to love ourself.

Being in the Now is a true gift that is earned during our life journey. Being there always — is a way to Dragon Energy ∞

**Continuing our 3 perennial questions —**

2) What am I doing here (on Earth now) ?
3) Where am I going ?

We each, our **Real Self,** which we also call our **Soul** is *always in evolution*. Key in our evolution is finding out more about how our Soul works, which means how **we** work. So how can knowing how our Soul *works* help us?

We have referred to the Mystery or the Divine Mystery. Answering the 3 perennial questions from above: 1) I am my Real Self, 2) I am alive here on Earth to explore the Mystery, 3) I am going forward by finding more about me, others and God.

What is the Mystery? Eventually, we can realize and conclude that **we** *are the Mystery* that we are exploring. It is the Self exploring itself. It is our Self exploring ourself by going within, into our inner life. We are our own Hero within our lifetime wherein we are continuing on a years-prolonged Journey or adventure. It is a remarkable adventure as Hero of our own life.

# The Journey **Awakens** the Soul

But just what does *Awakens* mean here?

We address and answer this key question and term throughout this book. Words fit here such as — **wake up, arouse**, **rouse**, **stir**, **stimulate**, **initiate**, **promote**, **mature** and **develop**.

We believe it fits all of these.

Countless people have tried to define our Soul. So, it is us, we who inhabit our Real Self/Soul who can best go within and find how to define it for ourself alone.

*Knowing yourself is the beginning of all wisdom.* —Aristotle

∞ **Barbara**: I didn't know I had a Soul before I had my near-death experience (NDE). Being an atheist until then meant I never had to question or search. Then I stepped out of this *lifetime*, out of this *body* and out of this *ego*. I experienced eternity where time was just a memory and all my beliefs that felt so safe – melted. When I came back here, I then knew a part of me that would continue after my body died.

When speaking publically about NDEs, a physician who specialized in eye surgery, told me about an experience he had as an intern during his first participation in a birth. He saw a ray of white light penetrate the mother's belly just before the baby's head crowned. When he told me this, our eyes met and we both said together that perhaps the baby's soul came in. We both questioned if a baby's soul comes and goes during a pregnancy.

I questioned (idea this) again when I met a woman who I knew was having twins. There were two small spheres of Light following her around at the meeting we were attending. I asked her and she became upset because she wasn't pregnant. But after she calmed down she told me that she and her husband were adopting and they had recently been told that the expectant mother had just been told she was carrying twins. I explained to her what I had seen and we both wondered if the babies were following her and not the birth mother.

If those of us who have extra sensory perception got together and observed pregnant women, perhaps we could get closer to some answers on the debate about when life begins? i.e. when does the Soul enter its body and stay? ∞

## What is *The Journey*?

**How does our Soul evolve?** We each *Evolve* (grow, develop, progress, and advance) by going on a Journey of and within our current life. Enter Dragon Energy now by studying it and living what the Hero Journey is for each of us. Here is one illustration among several we have found, simplified in text box (Figure 3.1).

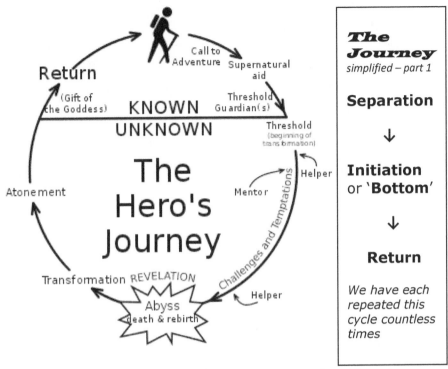

Figure 3.1 **The Hero's Journey** and outline ↑

We simplify the Journey as being in 3 parts: Separation, Initiation and Return. These generic parts are shown in other well-tested experiences — from Twelve Step programs to healing from our personal traumas to learning about and applying our personal Dragon Energy (Table 3.1).

**Table 3.1 Hero's Journey** — *Simplified- part 2*

| *Views* | *12 Step Story* | *Circle of Life* | *Comments* |
|---|---|---|---|
| *Separation* | What we were like | Life's traumas (see Chapters 14 & 15) | Learning about Dragon Energy |
| **Initiation /** Insight | What happened | Our 'Bottom' | Trying DE |
| **Return** | What we're like now | Psycho-spiritual insights/growth | Practicing DE daily |

## *Evolution* of the *Journey Concept*

In comparative mythology across human history, the *mono*myth is a common pattern of life actions and events found repeated in many stories. Joseph Campbell named it the *Hero's Journey*, and for decades there has developed a rich literature and following and much of it can be found online. The short version:

In his 1949 book *The Hero with a Thousand Faces* Campbell said: A Hero ventures forth from the world of common day into one or more trying situations. The Hero encounters difficult challenges, works through them and eventually wins a victory. The Hero comes back from this adventure with the power to give benefits to his peers.

In summary: we are each a Hero. We are each our *own Hero* on our own individual life's Hero Journey.

## Searching for Self and God

Phil Cousineau in the introduction to the revised edition of *The Hero's Journey* wrote 'the monomyth is in effect a **metamyth**, a philosophical reading of the unity of **mankind's spiritual history**, the **Story behind the story**'.

We believe that means Searching for Self and God. That healthy dynamic is what spiritual seekers pursue — who also want peace and occasional joy. We are at peace and joyous as we write this book.

Cousineau said,

*The journey of the Hero is about the courage to **seek the depths**;*

*the image of **creative rebirth**;*

*the **eternal cycle of change** within us;*

*the uncanny **discovery** that the **seeker is the mystery** which the*

*seeker seeks to know.*

*The Hero Journey is a **symbol** that **binds**,*

*in the original sense of the word,*

*two distant ideas,*

*the **spiritual quest** of the **ancients***

*with the modern search for identity.*

The biggest *survival* advantage we humans have is an ability to make and use tools of all sorts. Our human Mind is our basic and most powerful tool. A multi-tool has become a necessity for every survival kit, in every locale. We can each learn about Dragon Energy and use it as a tool to learning about our life and how to make it better.

## Do We Live Throughout Eternity?

From the large **Near-Death studies literature**, we know that while our body may die, from the documented reports of countless Near-Death Experiencers (NDErs), our Soul can — and likely will — live on indefinitely. We can extrapolate from the fact that these individual Souls lived beyond death to describe being on the 'other side of the life-death veil' and into God's unconditional love as the body dies. But they came back to consciousness to tell us what they experienced. All these research reports suggest that after death our Soul/Real Self/Consciousness continues to exist and evolve for an indefinite period of time. Possibly for eternity.

∞ **Barbara** Long before my NDE, as a child — when I was being severely punished, I experienced leaving this reality and waking up within or 'hanging out' in the tunnel that we NDErs describe.

Campbell expanded Hero stories from anthropologist Edward Tylor's works in 1871, Erich Neumann, the analyst Otto Rank and Carl Jung's view of myth. They described Gautama Buddha, Moses, and Christ in terms of the monomyth. The Hero's Journey first came to us with two documentaries: *The Hero's Journey: The World of Joseph Campbell* 1987 (plus his 1990 companion book). The second was Bill Moyers' interviews with Campbell, released in 1988 as the documentary *The Power of Myth* (and companion book).

When I became a teenager I had forgotten about it and numbed out from my trauma memories of abuse and neglect. But I remembered these experiences some 20 years later when I was in the tunnel during my life review in my NDE.

As I went on to do research and met others during my talks, I sometimes mentioned the childhood experiences out of my body and some others in the audience shared their out-of-body experiences during or after *their* child abuse. I even heard stories of women being raped and never being emotionally involved. They left their bodies and became bored with the violence. They turned away and some experienced seeing heavenly scenes. Those of us who have experienced this know our Souls. We know eternity.

Recently there has been a PhD dissertation on this called 'The Trauma/Transcendence Interface.' (Lehmann Dissertation 2010  ∞

We have many accurate reports within the NDE research of experiencers telling us what was happening outside of their body during their rescue or in the operating room or Emergency department. They tell us about conversations and details that there was no way for them to know otherwise. These reports are impressive and profound. What do they teach us?

Whether we believe it or not, our Soul/Real Self/Consciousness, can and — at these rare but real times — does *exist outside* of our *bodies*. Coming close to death is one trigger for these Out of Body experiences (OBE). We now have data on other triggers for OBEs: i.e., when a woman is giving birth, during detox from alcohol or drugs, experiencing tremendous loss, using a psychedelic drug, yoga, meditation, and even while assisting another in their death process.

Those reported time amounts for experiencing being outside of our body varied from a few seconds to several minutes. In some reports it lasted and was documented by medical professionals or credible others as lasting for *weeks* (e.g., in those published online and in the books and articles of Eben Alexander MD, Anita Moorjani, Jeff Olsen and Barbara Harris Whitfield).

When we are afraid to die, that fear comes from our ego. When we make peace with our ultimate death, we are in our Soul, not our ego. Our Soul has a peaceful quality about moving on to another reality. It is aware of the pain we may be experiencing. If it is pain that is not going to get better, our Soul welcomes leaving and becoming 'new' again. Our ego is what gives us all the arguments because it is terrified of disappearing.  ∞

## Connecting to God Strengthens our DE

We have said above that we strengthen our Dragon Energy by connecting to God. Doing that also makes our life go better. An *answer* to Perennial Question 3 *Where am I going*? includes re-connecting to where I came from. Assuming that we are each a child of God, we are returning to a more loving-connection to the God-of-our-Understanding. We connect through regular prayer, meditation and God-mindedness.

∞ **Barbara** Many years ago when I was visiting a Ronald McDonald House in Seattle, I consulted on a case with a 5-year-old child dying of cancer for over two years. He had recently told his doctors and parents that he no longer wanted chemotherapy and was ready to 'go.'

While this 5-year-old boy around the Ronald McDonald living room was playing, I tried to work with the mom whose hands were tightly wrapped around her chest and legs were crossed tight. In some 20 minutes he jumped up on his mother's lap and pushed hard on her shoulders until she fell back and her arms flew open. She finally cried and together we planned how she would tell her child that it was all right to go.

As I was getting ready to leave I noticed that the child had left and I found him lying in his bed. I reached out to touch him and he deflected my hands and put his hands on my temples. I was instantly transported into an altered state that felt very much like I was with him where he was at – and it was heavenly. I was in that state for the rest of the day. He died a few days later – peacefully with no more medical heroics. I felt and still do feel gratitude for knowing him that short time. He was pure Soul and after he placed his hands on my temples I knew for sure that he was going to be fine – with or without a body! ∞

### *A Course in Miracles*

For over 40 years we have studied and used the modern (1976) 3-volume *A Course in Miracles* to learn its great spiritual messages. Among its most memorable statements, it comments on our life Journey:

→ The **Journey** to God is merely the ***reawakening***
of the knowledge of ***where you are always***,
and ***what you are forever***.
[i.e., Safe in God's heart and mind]
It is a Journey without distance
to a goal that has never changed.
The Course later adds:
→ Teach only love, for that is what you are.

\*          \*          \*

In the next chapter we continue by expanding what we know about our Soul's Journey and how it relates to the *Circle of Life* and our developing Dragon Energy.

# 4  Our Journey and the Circle of Life

Caminante, no hay camino, se hace camino al andar.

Traveler, there is no path. *You make the path by walking*.

Antonio Machado

What is the Circle of life? On our journey from cradle to grave, we mark the most important moments of our lives with *rituals* and *ceremonies* around birth, birthdays, graduation, marriage and death. These life events, and often the emotions around them, are *universal*. Yet across the globe we perform them in different ways. But throughout the world from culture to culture there is a common use of the circle. This has been represented and symbolized in many ways — from art, drawings, paintings, tables and charts. Here is one example as the snake/Dragon biting its tail (Figure 4.1). We develop its origins and uses below.

### Our Journey and the Circle of Life

Over time we have used the circle to help us understand various aspects of our lives. These include the circle of the Hero Journey, which is also a way of representing the Circle of Life which *evolved from* the Gnostics, Alchemists, Hermeticists and who used the Ouroboros. These were previously regular people — ordinary — but were awakening spiritual seekers — who *thousands of years ago* identified with **our** also ordinary and awakening experience of searching for Self and God.

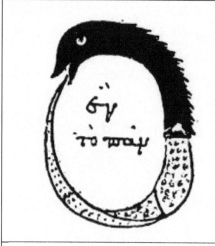

**Figure 4.1** The **Ouroboros** is a symbol of wholeness or infinity. The 17th c. scientist Isaac Newton (1642 – 1727) liked to look everywhere for how things worked. He often *looked under* conventional scientific assumptions, which led to many of his great discoveries. Ouroboros illustration with the words ἕν τὸ πᾶν, *hen to pān* ('**the all is one**'). 'The One, the All' and 'All-That-Is' are **other names for God.** See below and reference by Chambers 2018.

**Scientists rank Newton as being *equal to Einstein* in their important discoveries.**

## Circle of Life is Our Human Life Cycle

Biology as science rarely talks about the circle of life (recently made popular by the 1994 movie *The Lion King*, to be remade in 2019). Basically, a life cycle includes what stages an organism goes through from conception to death. We have also used circles to illustrate the long term process of healing from trauma, as being on our individual Hero Journey *repeated* as we heal as shown in *Healing the Child Within* (in the Figure on page 165).

## Looking for Truth and Meaning *Below the Surface*

From the earliest times we have looked for the truth of what is happening inside and outside of us and of others. Medical doctors and psychologists today look up and down for what is causing our problems. Attorneys look for legal ways to find truths to help their clients. Detectives from the fictional Sherlock Holmes to Monk look to uncover the truth. We have long searched below the surface for the truth as individuals and as groups.

Some 3,000 years ago — not trusting most people in the ordinary world — a few groups focused on looking below the surface for information to help them live better. Three groups who are millennia-old did that. These include the early *Alchemists, Hermeticists* and the about 1,000 years later *Gnostics* (who we address now and below on Alchemy and Alchemists on other pages: 60 and 188). Today when we know, understand and use their principles, they can still help us in our healing from our common life's traumas and search for Dragon Energy.

These out-of-the box thinkers were the greatest inner explorers of their time. They had to compete with the conventional religious majority. They rarely got respect from most academic and political thinkers until the early 1900s when the psychiatrist Carl Jung — also an out-of-the box physician, who was spiritual — wrote about and used *Alchemical, Hermeneutic* and *Gnostic* principles and more.

The **Ouroboros** is an ancient sign of eternity, symbolizing the endless succession of incarnations which form the wheel or circle of *eternal life*. It came from the *Gnostics* who were an early Christian group that expanded our view of us, Christ and God. They had a system of mystical religious and philosophical doctrines that combined Christianity with Greek and Oriental Philosophies.

**Gnosis** was a Greek noun for *knowledge*, especially *personal knowledge* attained from *personal experience* and which has been called wisdom. The Eastern Dragon is often shown focusing on a stylized pearl that represents wisdom, a symbol of spiritual perfection and powerful amulet (good luck charm).

Gnosis means an insight into **humanity's real nature** as **divine**, leading to the deliverance of *God's divine spark within humanity* from the constraints of Earthly and ego-oriented existence. *Gnosticism* is an originating and still modern name for a variety of ancient religious ideas and systems, Jewish-Christian thought some 2,000-years-ago originating in the first and second century AD/CE.

Some Gnostics divided the Ouroboros' body into light and dark portions, signifying that good and bad, perfection and imperfection, and bound together in *matter,* like day and night (fig 4.1 above). This is because Alchemical matter was and still is seen as a below-the-surface *metaphor* or representation for *one and all* — *embracing,* as in Yin Yang and related understandings of our psycho-spiritual condition and path.

## Jung on Alchemy

The psychiatrist **Carl Jung** was well-read, scholarly and spiritual.

Jung said 'When **the alchemist** [who was an early psychological and spiritual psychologist] speaks of Mercurius [Latin for mercury], on the *face* of it he means 'quicksilver' [what mercury looks like on a flat surface] (mercury), but *inwardly* **the alchemist means the world-creating spirit** [God/Goddess/All-That Is] *concealed* or imprisoned in matter.' i.e., **God is in us**. See chapter 6 Archetypes and Mee on Jung's Dragon page 87.

We can find that *Alchemist within* by exploring and practicing inside of our Inner Life (see pages 60, 188 and 191, chapters 14 and 15).

The Ouroboros was also a representation of **wisdom**, as was the pearl in the Eastern Dragon's focus. In many ancient beliefs, the tail-biting serpent is the world serpent, the world-encircling serpent of the Hindu religion and the Gnostic Christians, symbolizing the eternal path of the sun. A serpent has been involved from the Hebrew Bible/Old Testament Garden of Eden. There, we have three: man as Adam, woman as Eve, and the serpent/snake as a bad guy and/or a potential trickster.

Colliers dictionary expands and defines Circle of Life as Nature's way of taking and giving back life to earth. It symbolizes the universe being sacred and divine. It represents the infinite nature of energy, meaning if something dies it gives new life to another. Elain Pagels' classic book *The Gnostic Gospels* summarizes this mind, heart and Spirit-opening description that expands Judeo-Christian values.

Could the snake-as-trickster signify *another meaning* than the interpretation that the conventional understanding that the snake represented Satan? The perceptive and intuitive Gnostics *reframed* the evil serpent of Paradise into the benevolent and helpful Ouroboros, which they respected because they saw that it had planted in man's heart the *yearning for more psycho-spiritual knowledge* (see also figure on page 100).

From yet another perspective — we can reconsider another connection for the 3: Adam the man as equating to the Hindu Kundalini energy of intertwined serpents coiled at the base of our spine called the *Pingala*, Eve the woman as *Ida* and the snake as represented in Kundalini knowledge (page 100).

### *Serpent/Dragon as Guardian*

Many mythologists, authors and movie script writers describe the Dragon somewhere in their work as guardian. We discuss this characteristic in chapter 15 on page 157ff.

'A symbol of sacred knowledge in antiquity was a tree, ever guarded by a serpent, the serpent or Dragon of wisdom. The serpent of Hercules was said to guard the golden apples that hung from the pole, the Tree of Life, in the midst of the garden of Hesperides. The serpent that guarded the golden fruit ...and the serpent of the Garden of Eden ...are the same.' Straiton 2010

**The Gnostic Gospels** Some of the original 12 Apostles and a small number of other early Christian follower Apostles wrote non-canonical Gospels (canon = 'authoritative') about their observations and experiences with Jesus onto many ancient papyri (a *papyrus* is a primitive thick paper) that were previously unknown until in 1945 when an Egyptian peasant discovered them in a buried clay jar in a cave near Nag Hammadi in eastern Egypt.

These ancient (almost 2,000 years-old) hand-written documents were studied and published as *The Nag Hammadi Library* and came to be known as 52 authentic accounts of the words and sayings of Jesus and followers. They were known by the higher ranked early Christians who picked which books to include or not into the *New Testament*, but they did not include any of these. (See *The Gnostic Gospels* by Elaine Pagels and *The Gnostic Discoveries* by Marvin Meyer.)

### The Map is Not the Territory

The common experience that things are not always what they may seem to be was brought into the later 1900s by the Polish-American scientist and philosopher Alfred Korzybski who developed the theory of general semantics. His work described how human knowledge of the world is limited by both our nervous system and how we use language. Korzybski thought that people do not have access to direct knowledge of reality. Rather, they have access to perceptions and to a set of beliefs which human society has confused with direct knowledge of reality. He is remembered as the author of the dictum: 'The map is not the territory'.

→ In this book we outline the map.

→ You, and we, find and live the territory.

### Back in the Territory

→ Let's review what the territory is. It is US. Which includes?
  • You the reader.
  • We the writers.
• And everyone else. ~ It is the inner gold that the Dragon may guard and protect. It is US. Here and Now.

## Our Inner Gold

It is our God-given inner gold. We find our inner gold by humbly and boldly going under and through the 3 Veils — one — at — a — time. Doing these may take risking losing control. Going under the first Veil we let go of our attachment to our ego. No matter what, all that we do every minute of every day is watched and processed and experienced by one person — **I** — the experiencer and observer.  Here are the names we have called our self.

**Table 4.1 Six Terms for the Same Individual Human Consciousness that is *In Us*, As Us**

| Term | Definition | Comment |
|---|---|---|
| *Real Self* *True Self* | Our true identity, who we really are. Other terms below show its depth and personal power. | ego is not it. ego is only a helper, at best a kind of 'sidekick' |
| *Child Within* | Another name for our Real Self. Using this term helps us identify better with our vulnerable yet powerful Real Self, and how to stay safer. | Also called Inner Child. |
| *Soul* | Hillman 'where thought, image, and feeling interweave, yet it is not the whole Psyche. He says Christians see Soul as 'the transcendental energy in man' and 'the spiritual part of man considered in its moral aspect or in relation to God.' | Some expand to the totality of elements forming the mind (Merriam-Webster dictionary) |
| *Heart* | Some call it the center of the total personality, especially with reference to intuition, feeling, or emotion. Related to moral compass. | The emotional center, esp. vs mind (as center of intellect) |
| *Consciousness* | Awareness of one's own existence, sensations, thoughts, surroundings, etc. | Full activity of the mind and senses |
| *Psyche* Psychology = mind ~study | The totality of the human mind, conscious and unconscious. Psychology studies it. From ancient times, it represents one of the fundamental concepts for scientifically understanding human nature.  From Greek for *life* or *breath*. | Refers to the forces in an individual that influence thought, behavior and personality. |

And it is what happens and what we do with our life

and all that we experience on our Journey.

Which we have addressed in these 3 chapters

and throughout these pages.

*Negativity* is the opposite of Creativity.

*Being pretentious* blocks Creativity

*Being* politically correct *constantly* blocks Creativity.

All 3 block our Dragon Energy.

# 4.2 Our Journey and the Circle of Life
*...continued*

## Our 2 Circle Stories: Hero *or* Victim

In my book (CW) *Healing the Child Within* I showed the following figure that describes our Journey — as we can tell our story to safe others — fellow travelers in individual or group therapy or Twelve-Step group meetings. Here below is how I described it there in a figure and words.

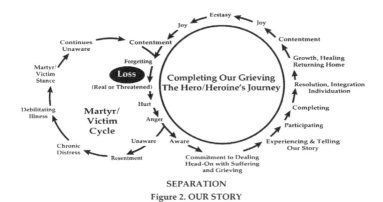

Figure 2. OUR STORY

**Figure 4.2.1 Our Story expanded,** including martyr/Victim cycle

© Charles Whitfield from *Healing the Child Within*

### These are our choices —

*Our own*    → **Be a victim or martyr** ... *or*

→ **Hero working through our conflicts and pain**

Our story does not have to be a classical AA (Alcoholics Anonymous) or NA (Narcotics Anonymous) 'drunk-a-log' or long in length. In telling our story — with safe people — we talk about what is important, meaningful, confusing, conflicting or painful in our life. We risk, share, interact, discover and more. And by so doing we slowly heal ourselves.

While we can listen to the stories of others, and they can listen to ours, perhaps the most *healing feature* is that **we**, the story teller, get to **hear our own story**. While we may have an idea about what our story is whenever we tell it, it usually comes out *different* from what we *initially thought*.

I have illustrated our story in Figure 4.2.1 above [the same as Fig 2 from my book *Healing the Child Within* p. 98]. Starting at the point on the circle at about 1 o'clock called 'contentment,' we can forget that we are in our story. For most of us joy is seldom and ecstasy is rare. Eventually in our day-to-day life we experience a **loss**, whether it be a *real* or a *threatened* loss. The stage is now set for both grieving and growing. In Figure 4.2 I have summarized most of the initial pain of our grieving as hurt. And when we feel hurt, we tend to get angry.

At this crucial point we have a possibility of becoming aware that we have experienced a loss or are suffering an upset. And here we can choose to make a commitment to facing our emotional pain and grieving head-on. We can call this cycle of our story a 'completed' one or the 'Hero/Heroine's journey.' Or we may remain unaware of the possibility of working through our pain around our loss or upset. We may then begin to build up a *resentment* (anger, dislike, upset) and/or to blame ourselves (shame, guilt), which eventually leads to stress-related illness, and to more prolonged suffering than if we had worked through our upset and our grieving in the first place. We can call this cycle the 'victim cycle' or the 'martyr/victim stance.'

If we commit to work through our pain and grieving, we then begin to share, ventilate, and experience our grief.

We may need to tell our story in such a fashion several times periodically over a period of several hours, days, weeks or even months — in order to finally complete our story. We may also have to consider it in other ways, mull it over, dream about it and even tell it again.

If you ever feel like a martyr or a victim, read chapters 14 and 15. A **martyr** is a 'victim' who *won't admit* to their victim role in perpetuating their martyr/victim stance.

\* \* \*

Several great creatives have related our Hero Journey through recent movies and their characters to stages or steps (Michael Mervosh (who founded the *Hero's Journey Foundation*), Michael Meade, Dan Bronzite, Scott Jeffrey and others – summarized in Table 4.2.1).

∞ I (BW) never understood the meaning behind the *Circle of Life* before my NDE. Perhaps we don't ponder such thoughts until we reach mid-life.

My near-death experience happened after back surgery in 1975 in a Stryker-frame Circle Bed. I was 32. Fast-forward to 1990. I was researching NDEs and I got an offer from the publisher Simon and Schuster for me to write a book. I named this first book *Full Circle*: The Near-Death Experience and Beyond. I didn't understand the significance of 'Full Circle' back then. I think I was at first unknowingly connecting it to the Circle Bed.

My Near-Death Experience started with my grandmother Bernice greeting me in 'the tunnel.' We embraced and re-experienced all 19 years we were together in this lifetime. I felt her loving warmth again that I had felt as a child, I saw and felt everything she did and I know she was seeing and feeling my love for her.

A week later I again left the circle bed — but this time I was not close to death. I had been forgotten about with my hospital room door closed. Than I had rotated onto my belly which was so painful that I screamed for help! This became a trauma in itself. I was crying until I lost consciousness here in this reality.

We hear this kind of experience as being a 'trigger' now more often. It is called 'The Trauma/transcendence interface.' It is a perfect example of Ciruelo's drawing of the Veils. I was helped by an amazing intelligent and compassionate Energy to revisit all 32 years of my life at the time.

Although I had always 'believed' that I was full of shame — because I was told that throughout my childhood, this incredibly loving and positive Energy let me see my life through Its eyes and heart. All of my memories 'flipped' from painful and punishing — to a healthy understanding of my parent's traumas and my innocence.

My 'full circle' didn't finally show itself until I became a grandmother. The same love I felt and gave to my grandmother is back again. I see it in my grandchildren's faces especially their eyes. The only constant on our journey is how we love ourselves, others and God. Our relationships can become an important part of our full circle in our Circle of Life.

I describe more on my story in *Eternal Circle of the Soul*

on page 185 just before the Glossary.

∞

## Table 4.2.1 Hero Journey Sub Stages and Movies Examples

| Journey Stage | Description | Examples |
|---|---|---|
| The Ordinary World | The Hero's starts | In the *Wizard of Oz* - Dorothy Gale living on her farm |
| The Call to Adventure | The Hero realizes that there is a larger world that he can be a part of | Harry Potter gets a letter from Hogwarts (*Sorcerer's Stone*) |
| Refusal of Call | In doubt, the Hero decides not to undertake the quest | Luke Skywalker tells Obi-Wan that he can't go to Alderaan |
| Meeting with the Mentor | First encounter with the Mentor figure or when Mentor encourages Quest | *The Karate Kid* Daniel LaRusso meets Mr. Miyagi |
| Crossing the First Threshold | The Hero moves from Ordinary World to the Special World, sees difference | *Fight Club* Narrator walks into Tyler Durden's house for first time |
| Tests, Allies, and Enemies | The Hero begins to undertake tasks that will help him prepare for the road ahead; meets friends who will aid and foes who will try to stop him | *Lord of the Rings* Frodo leaves Rivendell with the Ring Fellowship, and has to learn how to be on the road as he goes |
| Approach | Internal and external preparation; usually includes an imposing destination | *Matrix* Neo and Trinity gather an arsenal before heading off to rescue Morpheus |
| The Ordeal | The central conflict, the big boss fight, where death is imminent | Dorothy and her friends battle the Wicked Witch in her castle (*Oz*) |
| Seizing the Sword/Reward | Having slain the enemy, the Hero is free to take treasure; sometimes item of great value, as Holy Grail or person, but may be abstract, as end to a war | *The Hobbit* After the death of the Dragon Smaug, Bilbo and the dwarves are free to help themselves to his treasure |
| Enlightenment/ Apotheosis and Resurrection | Hero may need growth to peak and show itself at once in enlightenment (*apotheosis)*; this insight helps let go old ego-attached self; punctuated by a symbolic or literal death and rebirth. | In *Bill W*, Bill Wilson hits bottom in alcohol withdrawal delirium tremens. Prays for help from God, lets go of ego into spiritual awakening. Soon co-founds AA. |
| The Road Back | The *Special World* adventures and lessons may have become more comfortable than the *Ordinary World*. Returning can be harder. | After the One Ring is destroyed, Frodo has a hard time adapting to life as a normal Hobbit in the Shire (*Return of the King*) |
| Return with the Elixir and the Master of Two Worlds | The Hero returns home awakened, uses gifts and lessons learned to better others. Must come to terms with all of the personal changes and reconcile who he was vs who he has become | Now a Jedi, Luke restores balance to the Force, helping bring peace to the galaxy; soon able to resolve his relationship with his father and move on. *Return of the Jedi* |

At some point Awakening begins.

The awakening happens with trauma or it happens when somebody you love dies.
It can be drugs, it can be meditation, it can be a hymn, it can be a leaf falling, it can be lying under the stars, it can be trying to solve a problem where your mind gets so one-pointed it goes through the veil.

Whatever it is, you open up into other planes of consciousness that have been there in all of their splendor all the time. Ram Dass (Richard Alpert PhD)

# 5   The Power of

# Balancing Opposites

Your hand opens and closes and opens and closes.
If it were always a fist or always stretched open,
You would be paralyzed.
Your deepest presence is in every small contracting and expanding,
The two as beautifully balanced
And coordinated as birdwings.
— Rumi

Why do some opposites attract?
Why do some repel?
Why do some remain neutral or irrelevant?
What do we know from people who have studied them
over the millennia?
And how might it relate to Dragon Energy?

Difficult decisions can be hard to make. That is a common problem when we have 2 things that *are* the opposite of one another or *appear* to be opposite. I (CW) have written about this as being an important *Core Issue* in handling our relationships with people, places and things.

The issue here is **All-or-None** thinking and behaving.

Our choices are usually that we can
• pick one of the 2 opposite people, places or things *or* we can
• wait and see what happens.

Sometimes we can *attempt* to pick *both.* But we may get caught in a dilemma — where we would have been better off if we had picked one vs the other. Over the eons/ages/millennia, thinkers from the East have explored and addressed how to balance opposites in interesting and potentially creative and effective ways. First we will describe an Eastern approach.

## Eastern versus Western Approaches

The psychologist Richard Nisbett PhD writes that 'human cognition (i.e., thinking) is not everywhere the same,' that Asians and Westerners 'have maintained very different systems of thought for thousands of years' and that these differences are scientifically measurable. What do we know about all this? In this chapter we will first describe what we know about the history of the power of balancing opposites and how we can use Eastern *and* Western approaches.

This Power began to be developed within psycho-spiritual seekers in China and Tibet through their practice, writing and study about 2,500 years ago (500 BC/BCE). It is held within several sources, especially the *I Ching* — which is an influential text that has been read and studied throughout the world that inspires the worlds of religion, psychoanalysis, literature, and art. Eventually it took on an influential role in our Western understanding of Eastern thought and has given us another tool to healing from all kinds of illness and pain.

The interpretation of the readings found in the *I Ching* has evolved over millennia and recently over centuries of debate. Many commentators have used the book symbolically, often to give guidance for moral *decision making* as informed by Taoism and Confucianism. The hexagrams themselves have acquired expanded and cosmological significance and paralleled with many other traditional names for the processes of change such as Yin and Yang and Wu Xing (which include *The Five Elements* and more).

# The Yin Yang Symbol

The Yin Yang symbol was closely related, coming from Taoist and other philosophies. It has had a far-reaching influence in human culture. Its meanings contain the wisdom of ancient Chinese and Tibetan people and philosophers. The fundamental essence of the Eastern view of life is that 'The world is constantly changing and full of contradictions' (Nisbett, 2011 p 13).

The term *Dragon Energy* may have originated long ago in Taoism, a psycho-spiritual system evolved by Lao-tzu and Chuang-tzu advocating a life of complete **simplicity** and **naturalness** and of **noninterference** with the course of natural events. This ancient yet currently valid field of living and study has helped countless of us to gain a peaceful existence in harmony within **the Tao** (or simply *Tao*), which means **the Way**.

Yin and Yang represent two sides of the Taoist Universe *and* of our personal Taoist inner universe (which is **our inner life**).

Our own inner Yin and Yang dwell within us. Each has a partial opposing quality — and at the same time balancing each other.

**Yang** represents our positive, masculine, and active side.

**Yin** represents our negative, feminine, and passive side.

These have each been represented in countless ways by cultures worldwide, including as the serpents on the Caduceus used as a symbol of healing, which we describe in the section in chapter 8.

Similar to the Caduceus' Yang-equivalent (or masculine-equivalent) called the *Pingala* within the Kundalini spiritual space and the Yin-equivalent (or feminine-equivalent) called the

*Ida*. They are likely identical energies that we each carry — hidden or not.

The first meaning of the Yin Yang symbol is that Yin and Yang balance each other. They cannot exist independently without the other. They exist only because of each other. They exist because of their opposite side and because each is inside of the other. But each does so in a balancing of a lesser-enough amount than their main portion. The other meaning of Yin Yang is that both of them are energies and they have a mutual conversion between them. The universe is full of Yin Yang energy and without such energy there, no life would likely exist.

Figure 5.1 **Opposites, Energies and Examples**

| *Yin/Yang Tao Symbol* | *Energies* | *Examples* |
|---|---|---|
| | Yang = Positive, day, masculine, sun, active, hot, hard, logical | • Light v Dark<br>• Day v Night<br>• Up v Down<br>• Right v Wrong<br>• Protagonist v Antagonist |
| | Yin = Negative, night, feminine, moon, passive, soft, intuitive | • Good v Bad<br>• Dependent vs. Independent |
| | Solutions = Access, name, study, choose, balance and live the positive | ↓<br>Major *Core Issue*<br>**All or None**<br>thinking and behaving |

From the appearance of the Yin Yang symbol, we see the black swirl has a white dot and the white swirl has a black dot. 'The truest yang is the yang that is in the yin'. The Yin Yang symbol expresses the relationship that 'exists between opposing but interpenetrating forces that may complete one another, make each comprehensible, or create the conditions for altering one into the other' (Nisbett p 14).

## The Tao is Part of God

'*In the beginning was the Tao, and the Tao was with God, and the Tao was God.*' That sentence, the opening of the Gospel of John translated from the Chinese version into English, says it the simplest. The scholar Hieromonk Damascene does here what the Church Fathers of the first through fourth centuries AD/CE did with their ancient Greek heritage. He takes up the ancient spiritual wisdom of the Chinese and uses the insights of long ago to illuminate the New Covenant of the coming of Christ — the Tao, the Logos — in the flesh. *

Along the way, he shares with us an immeasurable wealth of spiritual treasures from the Church Fathers, the holy Orthodox elders of modern times, and the great and mysterious Taoist sage Lao Tzu. He provides one of the most focused, moving, and yet most concise explanations of Orthodox faith and spirituality I have seen. *In summary*: Christ is the **fulfillment of the Tao**. We are each a Christ living the Tao in our journey as our personal Hero — first and foremost — and for some of us family and/or community Hero. Safe within our healing Dragon Energy — we go with the Flow — One Day at a Time.

## Did Christ have Dragon Energy?

He did some things beyond the ordinary. For example, in 3 years of teaching he modeled how we are each a child of God, how to love self, others and God, how to talk with God, cut how we view historical time in half, and 2,000 years later dictated *A Course in Miracles* to Helen Schucman for us to learn more. Of all the great teachers and philosophers from his time and before him he was the most documented to have been alive than any other person. Some readers may have other ideas or positives. We authors are confident that we can identify that he had Dragon Energy of the Alpha Level.

perspectives

## Enter the Phoenix

Figure 5.2 **Phoenix ~Dragon as Opposites** and **Energies**

| *Phoenix Dragon Symbol* | *Comments* |
|---|---|
|  | Phoenix Yin Energy = Universal Divine Female Alpha Force (in white) Entropic change, Sensation /Feeling, Physical Materialization, Conservation, Potential, Regeneration <br><br> ~ *In Perfect Balance* ~ <br><br> Dragon Yang Energy = Divine Male Omega Force (in black) Intellect/Thought, Activation, Dematerialization, Conquest/ Control, Projection, Healing |
| Together, balanced, they can give us a more peaceful life. To do that we can use our now available Dragon Energy. ||

Could this Phoenix Dragon symbol below be a meaningful variation of the Yin Yang symbol by showing mythical creatures instead of colored geometric circles? We believe that it *validates* and *expands* the Yin Yang symbol's deep dynamic and meaning. Adding these lively representations extends our individual experience higher and deeper. Both Phoenix and Dragon fly themselves and thereby fly each of us high into the heavens as we negotiate our life's Yin Yang opposition paradox for us to consider.

The 2004 book *Christ the Eternal Tao* looks at Christ through the innocent vision of Lao Tzu. People of the modern West have — to a great extent – become jaded by Christian terminology and doctrinal constructions, yet many of them are drawn to the person of Christ Himself. This book seeks to develop not only a new way of seeing Christ, but also a new language by which to express His message, drawing from the enigmatic style and poetic language of Lao Tzu.

The **Phoenix** myth In Greek mythology, a Phoenix (ancient Greek: φοῶιξ, *phoînix*) is a long-lived bird that cyclically regenerates or is otherwise born again.

Associated with the Sun, a Phoenix obtains new life by arising from the ashes of its predecessor. According to some sources, the Phoenix dies in a show of flames and combustion, although there are other sources that claim that the legendary bird dies and simply decomposes before being born again. There are different traditions concerning the lifespan of the Phoenix, but by most accounts the Phoenix lived for 500 years before rebirth. Seven ancient authorities (Herodotus, Lucan, Pliny the Elder, Pope Clement I, Lactantius, Ovid, and Isidore of Seville) have contributed to the retelling and transmission of the Phoenix story.

In the historical record, the Phoenix 'could symbolize renewal in general as well as the sun, time, the Empire, consecration, resurrection, life in the heavenly Paradise, Christ, Mary, virginity, the exceptional man, and certain aspects of Christian life'.

**Fig. 5.3 The mythical Phoenix**
(photo © by Bettman/Corbis)
Unraveling the legend of the Phoenix is trickier than it might seem. The fabled bird is so thoroughly entwined in our culture that most people have heard of it, but no one seems to know much about it.

The legend-myth may have developed in ancient Greece and Rome, where the Phoenix was sometimes associated with the similar-sounding Phoenicia, a civilization famous for its production of purple dye from conch shells. Because the costly purple dye from Phoenicia was associated with the upper classes in antiquity and later with royalty, in the medieval period the Phoenix was considered 'the royal bird'. Shen T 2017

So what can we do with this information? To begin this chapter we had asked —

Why do some opposites attract?
Why do some repel?
Why do some remain neutral or irrelevant?
What do we know from people who have studied them over the millennia?
And how might it relate to Dragon Energy?

## A *Western* Approach to Balancing Opposites

In the above we described a mostly Eastern approach to balancing opposites. In the section below we will address balancing opposites through a *Core Issue* in living and in our relationships with our self and most other people, places and things — and with God. It is *All-or-None*. And it is common.

## All-or-None Thinking and Behaving

All-or-None Thinking and Behaving *drains* our Dragon Energy.

As we go about our business of everyday living we encounter opposites often. With needing to be in control, all-or-none thinking and behaving is also one of the first and most primitive of the core issues commonly encountered in any stage of living, problem solving or healing. It limits my possibilities and choices because it says that all I can want or get in any relationship with a person, place or thing is 'all *or* none.' Either All (or on a numerical scale = a 10) or none (a zero) — nowhere in between. But how often *have* I or *do* I ever get 'all'? If I get 'all' rarely or never, then what does that leave for me? It leaves me *None*. So with an all-or-none mindset, I may end up believing or feeling that I essentially have *no* choices.

We get stuck in all-or-none thinking and behaving when we remain attached to our ego/false self. The ego can make only walls, not set healthy boundaries. Walls tend to alienate others, in contrast to assertive healthy boundaries that often work better to get what we want. As I begin to live from and as my True Self, I can learn to set healthy boundaries and limits, which in turn will allow me many more choices in my life. With this new insight and understanding I can choose among any one or more of the many points along the many spaces across the all-or-none spectrum from zero to ten.

All-or-none is the ego defense against pain that therapists call *splitting*. When we think or act this way, we do so at either one extreme or the other. For example, either we love someone completely or we hate them. There is no middle ground. (This core issue is so ingrained into a part of our collective unconscious that I found some 24 published songs about it, such as in the musical *Oklahoma* 'With me, it's all or nothing...' and in another popular song 'All, or nothing at all'). We see the people around us as either good or bad, and not the real composite they are. We judge *ourselves* equally as harshly. The more we use all-or-none *thinking*, the more it opens us up to *behaving* in an all-or-none fashion. Both of these actions tend to get us into trouble and to cause us to suffer unnecessarily.

We may become attracted to others who think and behave in an all-or-none fashion. But being around this kind of person tends to result in more trouble and pain for us. We may have been attracted to them because our *parents* may have *modeled it* for us along with other kinds of family dysfunction. While all-or-none thinking can occur in any of these family situations, it can stereotypically occur for example often among fundamentalist religious parents. They may often be rigid, punitive, judgmental, and perfectionistic. They are often in a shame-based system, which attempts to cover over and even silence our True Self.

## Common in Addictions and Co-dependence

All-or-none thinking is similar to active alcoholism, other chemical dependence, co-dependence or other active addictions and attachments, in that it sharply and unrealistically *limits* our possibilities and *choices*. To be so limited makes us feel constricted, and we are unable to be creative and to grow in our day-to-day lives.

## Transcending and Balancing All-or-None

In looking within — into our Inner Life — we begin to learn that *most things in our life*, including our healing or recovery, are *not all-or-none*. They are not either/or. Rather, they are often parts of both/and. They have shades of gray, they are somewhere along the spectrum of the middle, a 3, 4, 5, 6, or 7 and not either a 0 (none) or a 10 (all).

All-or-none has several guises, manifestations or variations described in the psychology literature—as we summarize in Table 5.1 on the next page. Psychologists call these kinds of unhealthy thinking 'cognitive distortions' (or errors in thinking). And they call learning to *handle* and ultimately *let go* of these irrational defenses against pain by the term 'cognitive restructuring' (cognitive is psych-speak for *thinking*, and often expanded to include emotions and behavior). Read over and, if interested, study each of these guises of all-or-none. These 11 ways of seeing and further describing it expands our understanding of this *second most encountered* Core Issue that emerges in relationship conflicts and early in the process of recovery.

## Dragon Energy is About Balance

Sometimes deciding and choosing between All-or-None is smart and healing, as e.g., in some addictions as alcoholism or compulsive gambling. Those who choose *None* nearly always benefit by a much improved life.

We remember that our worst addiction is being attached to our ego. A solution to balancing opposites is to explore our choices.

~**All**. ~**None**. ~**Both/And**.

Or ~ *Somewhere* on their broad **spectrum**.

➔ **Of all the people you will know in a lifetime, you are the only one you will never leave or lose.**

➔ **To the question of your life, you are the only answer.**

# Table **5.1 Guises and Dimensions of All-or-None**

| Guise of All-or-None | Definition | Comment |
|---|---|---|
| **All-or-None** | Absolute terms, like "always", "every", "never", and "there is no alternative" | Few aspects of human behavior are so absolute |
| **Splitting** | Thinking and acting in extremes (e.g., good v bad, powerful v defenseless, and the like). | Can be seen as a developmental stage *and* an ego defense |
| **Over gener-alizing** | Using isolated cases to generalize widely | Limits our choices and our freedom |
| **Mentally filters out the positive** | Almost exclusive focus on negative aspects of something while ignoring the positive. | e.g., focusing on a tiny imperfection in a piece of otherwise useful clothing |
| **Disqualifying the positive** | Continually de-emphasizing or declining the positive for arbitrary, *ad hoc* reasons | *ad hoc* ("for this purpose") = task oriented |
| **Jumping to conclusions** | Drawing negative conclusions from little or no evidence. Subtypes: 1) *Mind reading* - Assuming special knowledge of the intentions or thoughts of others and ... | 2) *Fortune telling* – Exaggerating how things will turn out before they happen. |
| **Magnifying *and* minimizing** | Distorting aspects of a memory or situation through magnifying or minimizing them such that they no longer correspond to objective reality. "Making a mountain out of a molehill" | A subtype: *Catastrophizing* – Focusing on worst possible outcome (however unlikely) or thinking a situation is unbearable or impossible when it is really just uncomfortable |
| **Emotional reasoning** | Making decisions & arguments based on intuitions or on a *feeling* v. objective evidence | "I rely on my intuition or feelings too often" |

**PPT** = Person, place or thing

# 6    The Dragon as an Archetype

An **Archetype** is an idea, subject, image or motif that recurs throughout art, literature and culture. [**Arche** ref. beginning, origin, source of action, first principle / **Type** ref. Greek *tupos* meaning imprint or blow; the 'type' in the psyche, an inner mental image.] An archetype is something shared by the collective unconscious of one or more cultures.

The psychiatrist Carl Gustav Jung MD (1875-1961) and colleagues developed archetypal, analytical and spiritual psychology (also called *Transpersonal* psychology) and psychiatry. He was a peer of Sigmund Freud who was an atheist and did not believe anyone who had spiritual experiences. Jung believed that an archetype was a

- *primitive mental image* that was inherited from mankind's earliest ancestors and that an archetype is
  - *present in* the *collective unconscious*.

The **Dragon** as an **archetype** *was* and *is*

*such a* **prototype** *or* **initial image** *from which all*

*the various forms of Dragons throughout the world were based*.

## How Many Years of Historical Development ?

Many myths were formed well before some 5,000-years-ago (i.e. 3,000 years BC, which was the time when early humans first began to *write letters* by hand and eventually *sentences* for others to read.

Some 25,000-years-ago (i.e., 23,000 years BC) the earliest Egyptian myth was about Ra (Re) the sun god who was said to have travelled each night through the 'underworld.' While travelling through the underworld Ra reaches two open doors guarded by snakes, which over the millennia and then by some 5,000-years-ago from today (i.e., 3,000 years BC) became what we know as Dragons.

Based on this history from anthropology, mythology and earliest art history we can conclude and summarize that we have known of Dragons for *at least 5,000 years*. If we reason that our creation of Dragons has evolved from our earliest mythological interpretation of snakes in Egypt, we can postulate and assume that these primitive Dragons-as-snakes existed in our creative imagination from at least 25,000-years-ago.

Jump thousands of years to today and we find the snake/Dragon firmly inside our past 200 years as the Caduceus symbol for the professions of medicine and healing in chapter 8 (page 93) .

### Table 6.1 **Snakes → Develop into → Dragons**

| Creature | Time estimate | Comment |
|---|---|---|
| Snakes | 25,000-years-ago | Serpent/Dragon *Archetypes* may be from much older times |
| Dragons | 5,000-years-ago | |
| *Humans* Homo *sapiens* | ~300 (350 to 260) **thousand** years ago | Anthropologists believe that *artistic creativity* is *one* of the *hallmarks* of humans |

## Today and Recent Past

When we search TODAY online for Dragons we find *countless* sources and works directly *about* and *including* Dragons in **art**, **games**, **mythology**, **folklore**, **books** and other **literature**, popular **culture** and in **movies** and **television**. Are there any creatures or monsters that you know that come even close to being covered this much in as many genres in our fantasy world, science fiction and culture? And as symbols in the medicine and healing professions? *any creatures used*

The atheist astronomer Carl Sagan once remarked: 'The pervasiveness of dragon myths in the folk legends of many cultures is probably no accident'. He felt compelled to address the Dragon's similarity to the great reptiles of the Jurassic era and 'explain them away.' How could Sagan do this?

Peter Dickinson wrote, 'Carl Sagan tried to account for the spread and consistency of dragon legends by saying that they are *fossil memories* of the time of the dinosaurs, come down to us through a general mammalian memory inherited from the early mammals, our ancestors, who had to compete with the great predatory lizards.' So, Carl Sagan believed that we evolved not merely as our physical bodies, but also as our memories 'uploaded' from our mammalian ancestors. Sagan C 1977 *The Dragons of Eden*

In modern art and literature, the Dragon is almost always shown with four legs, a serpentine body and with wings. This is expected due to the influence of some world faiths and the conformity of artists over the centuries to this view. A Dragon image that endures is of the Chinese 'Lung' which has remained fairly true to the original despite successive generations. This is somewhat strange given the plethora of Dragon appearances and behavioral types in art and literature.

Unknown to many of us, four nations have placed the Dragon on their flag. These include Wales, Malta, Bhutan, and the Cayman Islands. Decades ago England countered Wales with a flag showing the same but a white Dragon, shown below. The modern association with a white (rather than gold or red) Dragon is referred to in Sir Walter Scott's (1771–1832) poem 'The Saxon War Song.' In 2003 during his enthronement at Canterbury Cathedral, Archbishop Rowan Williams wore hand-woven gold silk robes that showed the white Dragon of England and the red Dragon of Wales. In 2014 the Royal Wessex Yeomanry in British military adopted the White Dragon as the centerpiece of their new cap badge.

South Korea has the Yin Yang symbol as the center of its flag and Papua New Guinea, Albania and Montenegro have the Phoenix on their flags (see page 73ff for our discussion of these symbols).

Figure 6.1 **Flags of Wales** & Older **White Dragon** of **England**

| *Wales* | *England* (old version) |
| --- | --- |

The *guardian* Dragon, the *playful* Dragon, the *fire-breathing* dragon *all share* the same physical attributes — a cross between the Egyptian snake images and the Chinese lizards with the logical wings. The *fire*-breathing notion has been mostly discarded. It may have no real place in ancient mythology, though some kind of breath weapon remains in a few tales.

What we are seeing is the *merging* of the ancient archetypes into a *composite image* that resembles *all* of them worldwide.

Already hinted at in some representations, in this book we are adding and further developing two natural and real characteristics of this magnificent being: **energy** and **intelligence.**

## In Our Cultural DNA

*from*

*25,000*

The Dragon archetype that has developed over countless years and up to a half million years is now essentially encoded into our cultural DNA. As we each awaken to our own individual Dragon Energy we will use its healthiest characteristics to our physical, mental, emotional and spiritual benefit.

## The Jungian Dragon

In his scholarly online essay article, Laurence Mee writes 'Though an archetype as an imprint presupposes that there was an imprinter in the first place, Jung does not concern himself with this, rather he concentrates on the *image* within the collective unconscious that *dominates* when there are *no other rational thoughts*. The unconscious is said to modify the conscious. Jung's idea of the archetype as a Primordial Image required that it was at least *common to entire races or entire epochs*, the most powerful archetypes being common to all races at all times. It also required that the image was in close accord to the ancient myths and symbols. The ancient symbols were supposedly created from the collective unconscious to explain certain phenomena of the world, rational thought being impossible at that time.' (Our italics and bold)

Mee concludes: 'In coming to terms with the Dragon archetype, one must explore its influences over the conscious. This can be best done during symbolic play sessions where the active imagination can be left to roam. Jung was convinced of the *healing power* of *play* and the *imagination* through various media, and its ability to put people in touch with material that is ordinarily repressed. The fantasies thus produced are done so in controllable circumstances. The images these fantasies take are varied and unpredictable for during the state of **play** people are **able** to **imagine anything**. This can take the form of playful Dragons, Dragons doing things that are not in keeping with the Primordial Images. It is probably the best way in which to discover the influences that the archetypal image has over the conscious and rational mind; and in discovering the influences one can come to terms with them.' (Our italics and bold)

The archetype of the *good Dragon* brings us to its *healthy moral compass*. This is because most of its characteristics, especially its *self-confidence* and *intelligence*, it knows how to recognize and handle conflict personally and for the good of all of us.

Human *artistic creativity* is considered by anthropologists to be one of the *hallmarks* of modern *Homo sapiens*. They see this creative art as part of our unique human behavioral and cognitive journey into an interpretative world of symbol, representation, abstraction, and design. But a rare sea shell found in an ancient cave, after 21 researchers analyzed it individually, was definitely carved upon and was dated to an astounding 430,000 to 540,000 years old.

But that shell was carved upon by Homo *erectus*, one of our ancestors, *not* early Homo *sapiens,* who began around 350,000 to 260,000 years ago. In the publication *Nature*, Joordens wrote, 'What we think of as typically modern human behavior didn't suddenly arise, in spark-like fashion. Something like that seems to have been in place much earlier.' While the intent of that first artist is unknown, the shell design is similar to later etchings and rock art made by early humans. In the next chapter we explore how to find our Inner Energy and activate it.

# 7 The Power of Inner Energy

## - *Self-Directed*

Most of us want energy to use to *get things done* all day. We look for energy in and from *all kinds* of *people, places* and *things.* To start our day most of us use a mild stimulant such as caffeine or theophylline in coffee or tea. Way too many have to light up for a nicotine smoke or vape to wake up too. Some of us add other energizers, including: pain killer *opiates, heroin,* the stimulants *cocaine, amphetamines, Ritalin* and/or *alcohol* and *other drugs — legal* or *illegal,* including cannabis. Some of us use the '*process*' addictions of gambling, food, sex and relationship addiction (sometimes exciting and sometimes toxic), and more.

But these are all shortcuts — in that each one substitutes by using *them* instead of going within and finding our Real Energy. Of course, it is always our choice.

Instead, if we choose, we can generate our personal Energy by our self from inside our own natural creative awareness and consciousness. This Real Energy is a basic and important part of Dragon Energy. It is Self-*Identified,* Self-*Directed* and Self-*Initiated.* We can always start it when we decide at any time of our day.

Finding and using Energy is a way that we achieve in our life and how we grow and evolve. In this book we explore the phenomenon of psychological and psychic energy. We will also address how we can use it two ways: 1) in our inner life and outer life, and 2) in our relationship with our self, others and the God-of-our-understanding.

## Energy Sources

Where **can** we find energy? Day-to-day, where **do** we actually find it? How can any of our *energy sources* relate to Dragon Energy?

We have two basic and vital sources of energy to live: The Sun and food. The Sun is the crucial and essential source of energy for most of life on Earth. As a star, the Sun is heated to super high temperatures by the conversion of nuclear binding energy from hydrogen fusing in its core. This energy is ultimately released into space mainly in the form of powerful and life-giving radiant or light energy. Without it, we wouldn't exist as we do (see Table 7.1 below). We also know that to exist day-to-day our body and brain needs food as its physical energy source.

We humans and animals are naturally drawn to the Sun's radiant energy so much that we try to get it when we can — from lying on the beach to travelling southward to using sunlamps. Sunlight is crucial in two ways, by 1) Stimulating our internal vitamin D production from cholesterol when our skin is exposed to sunlight. In the dark of winter when we are sunlight deprived our body stops making vitamin D. Vitamin D deficiency causes health problems such as fatigue, low immunity, muscle and lower back pain, and mood fluctuations from low energy to depression, called the 'winter blues' or seasonal affective disorder (*SAD*). And 2) Sunlight suppresses the hormone melatonin made by our pineal gland, which is released to help us sleep when we are in the dark.

But these two basic energy sources are not what this book is about. What Dragon Energy is about *includes our own personal* faculties, abilities, and capabilities and desires to go inside our inner life (which contains our mind, awareness and consciousness). To get into that central part of each of us it takes *motivation* and *focus* to get-things-done.

Table 7.1 **The Spectrum of Energy Sources**

| Basic and Vital | | The Three Motivations | | | Dragon Energy |
|---|---|---|---|---|---|
| *The Sun* | *Food* | to Survive | to Achieve | to Grow | |
| Radiant energy | Bio-energy from nutrition | Mostly from ego | From Inner life pain and our personal creativity | From Inner life pain and creativity on our Hero's Journey | Includes & Transcends our other energy sources |

The skill we can use to go within is **introspection**, which often includes self-reflection, self-examination, and careful contemplation of our inner life. These things for us to get done are our *needs* (current and past) and our *choices*.

**Our Three Motivations** These important parts of Dragon Energy include our motivations to *Survive*, to *Achieve* and to *Grow*. As we summarize in Table 7.1 above, our motivation *to Survive* comes mostly from our ego. This is the only part of Dragon Energy that is useful from our ego when we may need it. Three healers — psychiatrist Carl Jung and the great Indian teachers Muktananda and Meher Baba summarized it in the clearest way we have found: "The ego is a *wonderful servant* but a *horrible master*." (Repeated from above)

The author Stephen Covey in *The Seven Habits of Highly Effective People* said 'Motivation is fire from within. If someone else tries to light that fire under you, chances are it will burn very briefly.' So we alone have to *self*-motivate to get what we want. Then we have to *stay* motivated until we have reached our goal.

Our motivation to achieve
and then grow
Commonly comes from our
• mental and emotional **pain**
that lights our fire
— and then it comes from our
• **creativity**.

We (CW and BW) have published on personal growth from traumas and PTSD. We are all on our own *Hero's Journey* which we addressed above in Chapter 3.

We can now summarize by *modifying* our chapter title from

**The Power of Inner Energy - *Self-Directed***
to
"
**Our own Inner Energy - *Self-Directed is* Dragon Energy**

Our own personal Dragon Energy includes and ultimately transcends all other Energy sources.

\*        \*        \*

In the next chapter we address how and why the medical and healing professions have long used a serpent in their medical Caduceus symbol which as we described in chapter 6 above evolved into a Dragon.

*Should be BC/BCE*

# 8  Why Is the *Serpent* a Symbol of Medicine and Healing ?

Is a Dragon a kind of serpent? A Dragon is a large, serpent-like mythical creature that appears in the folklore of *most cultures worldwide*. Beliefs about Dragons vary widely by region, but in Western cultures for some 5,000 years (since 3,000 (AD/CE)) they have often been depicted as winged, horned, four-legged and in some capable of breathing fire (AD = Anno Domini [year of our Lord] CE = Current or Common Era). In Eastern cultures Dragons are usually depicted as wingless, four-legged, serpentine creatures with above-average intelligence.

*italics*

Table 8.1  **TimeLine**: *Dragons in Art, Literature & Media*

| In Myth & Literature | Humans homo sapiens | Snakes | Dragons | Snake in Bible | Caduceus |
|---|---|---|---|---|---|
| Years Ago | **260** to **350 K** | **25,000** | **5,000** | 2,500 | 150 to 400 plus |
| Comment | Your ideas? | Open for your own investigation within YOU - see Kundalini | Double meaning | Gradual development |

*Homo* is *Latin* for human being, *sapiens* for 'discerning, wise, and sensible'.
The formers of modern paleontology (roughly living things before 11,700 years ago) used the terms 'dinosaur' and 'dragon' interchangeably for a long time.

**Why represent healing?** Why is a serpent or snake, which is usually a fearful symbol of harm, used intriguingly and paradoxically as a symbol of healing in medicine, nursing and the allied health and other helping professions?

### *Some reasons*:

- The original and classical symbol of medicine was the staff of with an entwining serpent (Figure 8.1).

- The serpent's *shedding* of its *skin* symbolized *longevity* and *immortal* life and it had an early use in the Hebrew Bible/Old Testament.

- The serpent's ability to change from a lethargic state to one of rapid activity symbolized the power to convalesce from an illness.

- Today many medical groups continue using it as a symbol. *Examples*: The *American Medical Association* has used it as its symbol since 1910; the *World Health Organization, the Royal Army Medical Corps*, *French Military Service, US Army Medical Corps since 1902*, the *Public Health Service*, the *US Marine Hospital* and more.

- In these ways the serpent has become and remains as a powerful symbol of healing.

But there is more. It has a deeper meaning.

## Its Inner Meaning

- The serpent Caduceus has an *inner meaning* that shows us an ancient experiential model (thousands of years old) that underlies and supports the Dragon Energy from a psychological and spiritual perspective. The inner meaning is from the whole Kundalini system which we describe in several sections below.

| Original Staff of Aesculapius | Caduceus |
|---|---|
| 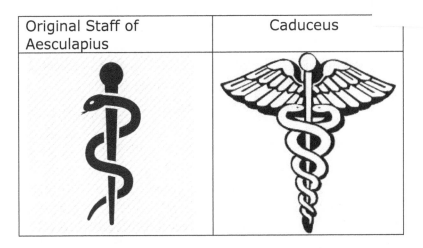 | |

Figure 8.1 **Development of the Original Aesculapius Staff into the Caduceus Staff of Hermes**

### Why the Wings?

Most Caduceus symbols also have a pair of **wings** at the staff top, as shown in Figure X above. A pair of wings is symbolic of the Greek god Hermes' speed (he was the messenger of the gods and his Roman counterpart was Mercury who had wings on his feet). Over time these two names came to be recognized as designating one and the same mythical being representing speed.

*space*

Western Dragons have wings to take them —and symbolically to *raise us* — high into the air above the Earth to get a view of what is most interesting and important below. This high flying air Dragon represents our conscious mind and our higher connection to God/Goddess/All-That-Is.

By contrast, the Eastern Dragon usually has small or no wings and is commonly a water dweller. Water here represents our unconscious mind — what we may not know fully or at all. In Chinese Taoist philosophy, water also represents intelligence and wisdom. Water is flexible yet strong, flowing yet still, calm yet dangerous. For Water, the surface is only the beginning, with the real movement hidden in its depths. Possibly unrelated, we humans are made of about 60% water.

*In summary*: The use of the symbol is puzzling because — How can harmful creatures be used to represent healing? The answer lies in the snake's characteristics of

• Its skin shedding as representing immortal life, as well as
• When appearing to be immobile its sudden change in activity that also emphasizes a sudden healing from sickness to a cure,
• Its reference early in the Hebrew Bible/Old Testament,
• It was used by Aesculapius who is the mythical god of healing, and *worldwide for over 150 years*
• Medical groups continue using it as a symbol of healing.
• The serpent Caduceus has an *inner meaning*, which we continue to describe below.

**More on Caduceus Inner Meaning:**  This 'serpent' Energy that is recognized in the Western medical symbol of the Caduceus shows us *symbolically* that balance and healing can happen with the help of this natural Energy inside of us.

The serpent Caduceus shows us an ancient experiential model that underlies and supports the Dragon Energy we are describing in our body, mind and spirit. It is an ancient (thousands of years old) representation developed by countless people in pursuit of healing within a variety of ancient and current psycho-spiritual practices. These healing aids include *meditation*, *Yoga,* acupuncture and *related practices* within the traditions of the Indian religion Hinduism, Chinese Taoism, Tibetan and Japanese Buddhism, in alternative medicine and originally psychologically adapted to the Western mind through the work of Carl Jung, James Hillman and others.

In the Caduceus the two opposite-facing serpents winding up the central column (the spine) cross over each other at the same points as the *chakras*.

**Chakra** is a Sanskrit term for wheel or circle. A chakra is an energy center that runs along the spine and up to the brain that is said to connect organs and physiological systems. The chakra system has 7 main chakras which are also analogous to Levels of Consciousness which we discuss below and relate both to our human Energy.

What could all this seemingly extraneous information mean to anyone who might be interested in Dragon Energy? What is a chakra? What is Kundalini Energy (Kun-dah-lee-nee)?

In Table 8.2 below we summarize 6 key terms related to the Caduceus and healing through its symbolically represented Energy that will help us better understand DE.

Look at the table below and study the six (6) unusual terms (to most of us in the Western hemisphere) and their meanings. Then after the table we say more to *help clarify* this system as an ancient and accepted *example* of *what Dragon Energy might mean* to us today.

Bear with us as we explain some of these outside-the-box psycho-spiritual terms.

### The Energy Present in All Living Things

The ancient Yoga science texts described a life energy present in all living beings called *prana*. Corollary Energies have been identified in many cultures, such as *chi* and *huo* of Tibetan yogis, *quaumaneq* of Eskimo shamans, *incendium amoris* and *photismos* of Christian mystics. So there are many spiritual names for this generic Energy that is in us as us. In the *Eastern* and some Alternative Medicinal Models health is achieved by working with this Energy in Acupuncture, Yoga and Tai Chi. In the West we use several energy-giving methods.

## Table 8.2  6 Terms Summarize Caduceus & Healing Energy

| English | Sanskrit * Term | Description | Comments |
|---------|-----------------|-------------|----------|
| Energy and Growth *Centers* | Chakra / Chakras | Symbolized in spaces between coiled serpents | Also called *nadi* chakras that parallel Levels of Consciousness (pages 93ff & 214) |
| Energy and Growth Path/*Chanel* | Nadi see 3 more Major Nadi paths below | Channels through which healing prana and Kundalini energy flow | Memorizing these 6 terms helps us understand subtle healing |
| Central *Energy Path* | Sushumna | Connects base with the crown chakra | Vertical, stabilizing, grounding core |
| Left coiled path | Ida 'Comfort' | Feminine, introverted, lunar right hemisphere | Yin, emotional, subjective, internal |
| Right coiled path | Pingala 'Golden' | Masculine, extroverted, solar, left hemisphere | Yang, rational, objective, external |
| Psycho-spiritual Energy | Kundalini *Kunda* is Sanskrit for *coiled* | Generic Energy in many if not all religions. Other names for it: *Holy Spirit*, *Great Spirit, Ruach ha...* | *Kadosh,* sometimes called *Serpent Energy* and we now add *Dragon Energy.* |

Starting at the bottom of the table above, **Kundalini** is one name for the generic Energy that can be found in the heart of many if not all religions. Other names include: The *Holy Spirit*, *Great Spirit*, *Ruach ha Kadosh* (within the esoteric Hebrew *Kaballah*). See pages 213 -214 for more details.

With all due respect, when we combine Dragon Energy with God's Holy Spirit we are here introducing *Dragon Energy* as another way to help understand the *Serpent Energy* of the medical Caduceus.

* The **Sanskrit language** of ancient India with a 3,500-year history peaking around 600 BC/BCE, is of a wonderful structure; more perfect than the Greek, more copious than Latin, and more exquisitely refined than either, yet bearing to both of them a stronger affinity, both in the roots of verbs and the forms of grammar, than could possibly have been produced by accident; so strong indeed, that no philologer (language student) could examine them all three, without believing them to have sprung from *some common source*, which, perhaps, no longer exists. *William Jones, 1786, quoted by Thomas Burrow in The Sanskrit Language.*

This Kundalini energy force and power is represented *symbolically* as a serpent, resting in a coiled base three times around the spine. These terms in the table and below are from the original Sanskrit language of some 4,000 years ago from 2020 (which is also 2,000 years BC/BCE) and are derived from Indian Hindu Yoga science.

**Nadis** These nadis are identical to the parts of the caduceus. When activated, this healing Kundalini force travels through three *channels* of *growth canals* called *nadis.*

The first nadi, called the *sushumna,* in the *staff*, is vertical and straight, traveling in a parallel motion with the spine.

The **Sushumna** is the vertical *central energy path*, the stabilizing and grounding core, connecting the base with the crown. Each of the chakras is situated along the column of the sushumna symbolically contained within the two serpent coils. Kundalini energy moves upward through this pathway.

This **Kundalini healing pathway** makes the way for the ascent or rising of Kundalini energy which moves up through it. The energy is said to be activated by the two coiled serpents or nadis called Ida and Pingala which work together in polarity and duality, similar to the Yin and Yang.

*Ida* is the left coiled channel that means 'comfort' in Sanskrit. It represents feminine, introverted, right hemisphere, lunar energy, subjective, internal and emotions.

*Pingala,* on the other side, is the right coiled channel. It is associated with masculine and solar energy as well as mental and physical endeavors. Pingala means 'tawny, brown, golden', or 'solar' in Sanskrit.

Kundalini energy has the potential to activate when both of these *nadis* are in balance with each other. The two channels twist together like that of the two serpents, intersecting at several points, or *chakra* energy *growth centers*. We describe the 7 chakra centers in some detail and how they relate to Dragon Energy in the Appendix on page 214.

So most religions and cultures have named these terms for this universal energy that is in all of us. In the Eastern Medical models health is achieved by working with this energy in acupuncture, yoga, in some forms of meditation and Tai Chi.

Figure 8.2 **Mythic Depictions of the Medical Caduceus Symbol**

From the master transpersonal artist Alex Grey.
(Interesting comments by Mynzah as shown)

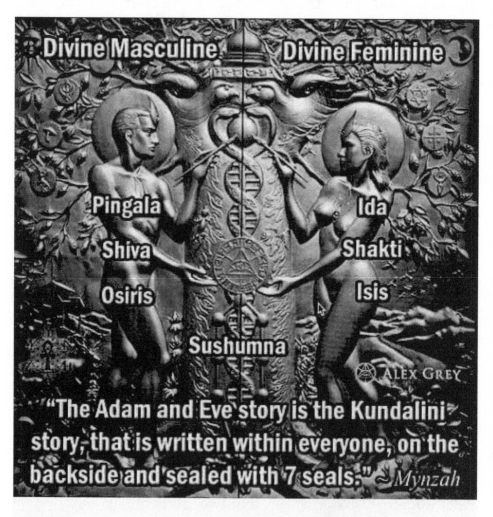

# 9  The Power of Spiritual Awakenings

Have you had a spiritual awakening? Or do you wonder if you might have had one? A spiritual awakening is an *experiential* opening to a *power greater* than *our self*. As a result, we become more aware of and open to our Real Self, others and the God-of-our-Understanding.

Over the last 40 years I (CW) have taught countless day-long workshops on healing from traumas and addictions. Based on informal surveys that I did on these recovery-motivated people, I estimate that at least one in three (of these certainly) people have had a spiritual awakening of some sort. Perhaps 1/4th of those spiritual awakenings were triggered by near-death experiences. The remaining 75 % are triggered by numerous other experiences, from meditation, to childbirth to "hitting bottom" in a critical or desperate life situation. Some of these events have activated some people to experiencing the Kundalini (Kun-dah-lee-nee) Energy process of spiritual awakening.

*Who or what* is it that actually *does the awakening*? Is there a part of us that begins to become more aware and opens us to our self, others and the God of our understanding? Our sense is that it is *common* for a spiritual energy that *begins to awaken us* to our *Real* or *True Self* (the key to Dragon Energy), and helps us learn about our ego or false self.

*Kundalini* is a kind of cultural and spiritual name for the generic Energy talked about in most world religions. Eastern medical models incorporate this energy into their healing modalities, i.e., in acupuncture, yoga and some forms of energy massage. Many people who work with the energy compare it to the Christian *Holy Spirit*, Native American *Great Spirit*, or the Hebrew term *Ruach ha Kadosh.* We believe that these are all terms we have given to the same *unconditionally loving Energy* of God. We believe that this Energy is also a key part of *Dragon Energy*. All we have to do now — to strengthen our Dragon Energy — is to connect experientially to the God of our understanding.

**Near-Death & other Spiritually Transformative Experiences**

Spiritually Transformative Experiences (STEs) are occurring with increasing frequency to some Westerners who had never heard of it and had done nothing consciously to stimulate or arouse it. It has been experienced as sizeable rushes of energy through the body. This Energy can create profound changes in the structure of our physical, mental, emotional and spiritual lives. I (CW) was one of these Westerners who experienced it unexpectedly one night when I was at a most painful bottom mentally and emotionally, which I will now describe.

**My Kundalini Experience** as an example: I (CW) had lived alone in Baltimore for 20 years. Mid-way during that span in the spring of 1984 I had unexpectedly lost my job after 8 years teaching at a medical school due to the arrival of a new department boss who brought his own teaching staff. It had been my career and a livable income source. I was then 46 years old and still mostly an atheist.

When I was told of this shocking decision it was 10:30 at night. I was alone and lying in bed. Not knowing what to do, I felt devastated and the most afraid and hopeless I had ever experienced.

I had never been into praying for anything. While lying there in bed, in desperation, I closed my eyes and went within. I said to myself and to anyone who could be listening 'If there is a God out there — please help me.'

Within seconds to a minute I felt a series of some three or four warm and pleasant physical vibrations run up my spine, from my hips to my head. I shortly fell asleep and awoke the next morning refreshed and optimistic that I would find a source of income. Over the next months I went on to form a new private medical and therapy practice. The next year in 1985 I wrote *Healing the Child Within* which became and remains a good seller in the field of trauma psychology.

Two years before that I had sought out acupuncture treatment for my neck and back pain with an acupuncturist named Erica Lazaro in Columbia, Maryland. Within a few days of that experience, when I was at my next acupuncture appointment, not knowing what to call it, I described it to her in these same words.

She said, "Do you know what Kundalini is?" I didn't. I looked it up and now 35 years later at age 81, I am writing this account of my Kundalini experience, which I have never forgotten. Previously an atheist, since 1974 I had also begun to meditate and study the Twelve Steps of AA. I have since written 15 published books on addictions, trauma and healing, most of which include sections on the **usefulness of spirituality in healing**.

So I had already been meditating almost daily since 1974 and then getting acupuncture treatments since 1982, both of which may have been factors that helped me have my Kundalini experience.

One of the positive effects of having such an experience is a resulting series of opportunities for psycho-spiritual growth. For me these were also Synchronicities, which I will recount below as a prequel and blending from our chapters 12 and 13 on examples of our authors personal Synchronicities.

## Synchronicities Continue in my Hero's Journey

1) In 1974 living in Springfield, Illinois I had just learned transcendental **meditation** and began practicing it twice a day. (I lived there for 4 years teaching Internal Medicine and Addiction Medicine at Southern Illinois University School of Medicine.)

2) While there I first learned about the importance of the **Twelve Steps** of addiction recovery while teaching about addictions and attachments to Medical students. At that time we had been *one of the first* to have an organized *required class* for each student to *observe an AA meeting*.

3) Then in 1976 I was recruited to teach at the University of Maryland School of Medicine and moved to Baltimore, Maryland where I also began studying **A Course in Miracles** (ACIM). Studying *the Course* was the most compelling, engaging and freeing action I had ever done.

4) 1984 **my Kundalini** experience (described above), Baltimore/Columbia, Md. *Lost my job*, and *hit bottom*, first time in years I prayed to God and had an immediate *Kundalini experience.* In 1986 I wrote *Healing the Child Within*. In it and in later books I always included *spirituality* as a healing aid.

5) I *first* **met Barbara** in 1985 at a conference on consciousness, death and Near-Death Experiences.
We communicated a few times by mail and phone for 5 years.

6) Five years later I see her on TV April 20th, 1990, I call her to say I will be speaking on 'Feelings' to an *Adult Children of Alcoholics* conference audience in Connecticut. We meet then and two weeks later we started dating long distance.

7) I gave a two day workshop in Harrisburg PA. Invited Barbara to attend who then saw my research blending into hers. We start and maintain a growing relationship.

8) We move to Atlanta in 1996. In 1997 I joined the original **Adverse Childhood Experiences** (ACEs) study team at the CDC and outside continued my private practice. Wrote and published 8 papers on ACEs as a member of the ACE Study Team.

9) Barbara and I establish *Muse House Press* to publish our books without the censorship common among most publishers.

10) I attend Dragon Con in Atlanta in 2010 and we meet Ciruelo in 2015 who was also the featured artist for Dragon Con program cover (shown on page 144).

Our synchronicities continue — as we learn about the *Myth* and *Reality* of Dragon Energy ... and more ... day by day.

∞ I (BW) have been researching Kundalini now for 36 years when in 1982 I first met Ken Ring PhD who had suggested that I look into this term of Kundalini. All of the spiritually aware experts I have read, met or listened to agree that this basic, natural, and God-given energy is a major hidden trigger and process for us humans to evolve in our personal growth and consciousness.

### Barbara's Synchronicities in her Hero's Journey

My (BW) two Near-Death Experiences happened in 1975. One synchronicity led to another. Ten years later in 1985 I was hired as a research assistant to psychiatrist Bruce Greyson MD studying the after effects of near-death experiences at the University of Connecticut Medical School. I attended and was a speaker at many conferences for researchers studying this newly awakened bio energy for six years.

We found that *other intense experiences* had been documented to be closely associated with and result in what Greyson, Ring, I and spiritually interested others would eventually call a *Spiritually Transformative Experience (STE).* Being interviewed by Ken Ring sent me searching into the writings of Lee Sanella

MD, John White and Itzak Bentov and helped Greyson, Ring and I to expand into the term *Physio-Kundalini Syndrome.*

I met Ken Ring in 1982. Within a year of our interacting, I became a key subject in his 1984 seminal book on near-death experiences *Heading Toward Omega.* His hypothesis (and my experience) is that this is a *strong* and *important* energy awakened or aroused in an NDE. What is more, countless other spiritual seekers were becoming increasingly aware that — when aroused, awakened or activated — this is a seed planted for this Transpersonal Energy to continue to spiritually awaken us gradually over our individual and collective life time that we have remaining on this planet.

## Triggers for a Spiritual Awakening

How many of us have experienced this Energy? We found that other intense events than having an NDE could start or trigger having a *Spiritual Awakening.* These other experiences, besides being close to death included

- Childbirth,
- the loss of a loved one,
- bottoming out from a painful loss,
- while using a psychedelic drug,
- during alcohol or drug withdrawal,
- in meditation, Yoga, or
- some with acupuncture treatments, as mine (CW Kundalini experience) above and
- spontaneously for some. Later we found that a
- 'fear death' experience could also trigger having a Spiritual Awakening (e.g., someone was in a severe accident and thought they were going to die). When it was over, they didn't get hurt, but the fear still triggered a transpersonal experience (in transpersonal psychology this has been called the 'Trauma/Transcendence Interface').

# Review Summary of Terms on Our True Identity

Here we review the summary from page 63 of the terms we have used over the recent 100 years to describe our True Identity. These are each useful names for our **mind**.

## Table Summary **Six Terms for the Same Individual Human Consciousness that is our True Identity that is *In Us*, As Us**

| Term | Definition | Comment |
|------|-----------|---------|
| *Real Self* *True Self* | Our true identity, who we really are. Other terms below show its depth and personal power. | **ego is not it.** ego is only a helper, at best a kind of 'sidekick' |
| *Child Within* | Another name for our Real Self. Using this term helps us identify better with our vulnerable yet powerful Real Self, and how to stay safer. | Also called Inner Child. |
| *Soul* | Hillman 'where thought, image, and feeling interweave, yet it is not the whole Psyche. He says Christians see Soul as 'the transcendental energy in man' and 'the spiritual part of man considered in its moral aspect or in relation to God.' | Some expand to the totality of elements forming the mind (Merriam-Webster dictionary) |
| *Heart* | Some call it the center of the total personality, especially with reference to intuition, feeling, or emotion. Related to moral compass. | The emotional center, esp vs mind (as center of intellect) |
| *Consciousness* | Awareness of one's own existence, sensations, thoughts, surroundings, etc. | Full activity of the mind and senses |
| *Psyche* *Psychology = mind ~study* | The totality of the human mind, conscious and unconscious. Psychology studies it. From ancient times, it represents one of the fundamental concepts for scientifically understanding human nature. From Greek for *life* or *breath*. | Refers to the forces in an individual that influence thought, behavior and personality. |

Having grown up in a dysfunctional family, to survive we had to explore how to handle our emotional and physical pain. We had to learn what *creativity* was and meant. In the next chapter we address that important power that comes with Dragon Energy.

How to Boost DE

⊏ Preface

Glossary

Index

# 10   The Power of Creativity – *part 1*

Among the 16 characteristics of Dragon Energy (listed on pages 23-24), *Being Real* and the *Being Creative* may be the most useful for we humans to use to make our life go better. Remember that Creativity is our **mind's strongest quality** and **most productive life skill**. It is a key part of Dragon Energy. We show and describe and discuss the mind on page xxvii in the *Introduction*. Technology and creativity author George Gilder said that the human mind is the ultimate creative force and that it comes to each of us in the image of our Creator.

When creativity is flowing through us, any physical or emotional pain disappears. We have boundless energy and the associated FLOW-state replaces any distractions both inside and out.

Creativity makes the ordinary into the *extra*ordinary. It is the process whereby in any area of our life we make something new or better (a product, solution, artwork, design, literary work, approach or the like) that has value. What counts as being 'new' may depend on the *individual* creator, or on the *society* or *space* within which the novelty occurs. What is 'valuable' is similarly defined in various ways. Being creative, we make a novel, useful product.

Our experience is that the **creative process** involves six basic parts:

• Inspiration,
• Perspiration (the hard work of putting together the nuts and bolts of any creative process),
• Imagination,
• Freedom,
• Healthy self-care, and
• Humility.

**Inspiration and Perspiration**   In our experience with the creative process we have learned that we nearly always need two things to produce anything new: *inspiration* and *perspiration*. The inspiration can be an *invigorating idea* that can make an original contribution to all who may read or use it. But that kind of inspiration necessary for our writing has not always been easy for us to find.

Since we have written and published some 22 books and over 60 articles, in this book we will use writing as a primary creative product example. I (CW) have also painted a few realistic oil paintings, so I will occasionally use painting as a secondary example. Of course there are many more areas of creative endeavor, and the principles for creativity we describe will be essentially the same for most.

• *Inspiration,* Latin *inspirare*, meaning 'to breathe into' or 'breathed upon.' The Greeks believed that inspiration came from the Muse and gods. The Ancient Norse religions saw inspiration as coming from the gods, such as their Odin. Inspiration is also a divine matter in Hebrew poetics. In the *Book of Amos* the prophet speaks of being overwhelmed by God's voice and compelled to speak. In Christianity inspiration is a gift of the Holy Spirit. These give different names to the same thing. In this book we will often call it the Muse.

• Inspiration may come because the creative person tunes to their previously unconscious, divine or mystical 'breath' or 'winds.' Inspiration may also come out of unresolved childhood or later trauma or psychological conflict. In this respect inspiration can come directly from the unconscious or subconscious mind.

Aware psychodynamic psychologists saw artists as fundamentally special and at the same time wounded in this way which can eventually be reframed as a *gift* — otherwise they would not likely have been so creative. Today modern psychology seldom studies it, but sees it as an entirely internal process only. In each view, however, whether empiricist or mystical, inspiration is, by its nature, beyond our ordinary rational control.

∞ Many years ago, I Barbara, was having trouble with a life experience and so I put myself back into psychotherapy. Half the battle while working something out in therapy is finding the right therapist. I prayed hard on that and it worked. She listened carefully as I explained what this experience had brought up from my past and it boiled down to something I described as the size of a pea that was broadcasting a nasty negative voice (before blue tooth speakers but like one). I identified it as all the negativity from my childhood especially my mother's voice. I wanted it out! She explained that there was a great use for that deep haunting, because when I made friends with it – it would help me with my writing. And she was right. It does! ∞

**The Muse** is a key part of our inspiration. She is the goddess of creativity, an otherworldly creature inspiring the artist before and while at work. She has usually been portrayed as a Being who is outside of us. The Albert Brooks movie 'The Muse' and our writing experience remind us that the best Muse lives *inside* us if we will only heed her calls. As is so about Dragon Energy, the Muse is both a Myth and a Reality.

She usually can't be forced. She waits while our ideas come up, hibernate, percolate and develop. As we wait, often frustrated, we may remind ourselves that we need more substance (e.g., research, practice, imagination, notes to ourselves). What we are about to write or do next may be something new, but to us still unknown and incomplete.

Then one day The Muse appears — slowly or quickly. She moves into our thoughts, minds, and hearts. She has been there most of our life, and through our waking and sometimes our sleeping hours. What we then write, draw, paint or craft ideally will flow smoothly. And sometimes it goes laboriously but appropriately slow.

She sometimes synthesizes, taking various parts from other ways to do things and creates a new way. Everything we have studied and enjoyed learning about becomes bits and pieces to a new puzzle we create.

At times, we've had great ideas that went nowhere. Sometimes they lay dormant, only to resurface later. Other times, we got inspired enough about something that we then build up enough creative energy to begin the long process of writing an article or a book. Or of painting a new canvas. Or any other endeavor.

∞ The hardest part for me (Barbara) used to be getting me to the blank page with a pen or the keyboard. I didn't feel worthy. I argued with myself. Then I started praying as I sat down in front of my keyboard and screen. I asked for help so this writing could help other people. Now, 12 books later, I know I am open to be joined by an invisible intelligence that will add or turn my thoughts onto another path. Sometimes, I don't even know I knew that! It feels like I am walking on sunshine. ∞

• **Perspiration**  To do the actual writing or painting, we need more than inspiration. We also need *perspiration*. This means I need to make myself to sit down, put pen to paper (or fingers to keyboard or voice to recorder, or paint to canvas) and write until I've accumulated enough good words. Because I (CW) write nonfiction, in preparation for any new piece I have to do a lot of reading as research.

Perspiration is the day-to-day, month-to-month, and sometimes year-to-year hard work that we writers and other creators need to complete a project. Thomas Edison said it best: "Genius is 1 percent inspiration and 99 percent perspiration."

When it happens, I use and enjoy the creative inspiration the Muse inspires in me. But the Muse can't usually work alone. In some ways, perspiration — the *hard work* — is the only one of the two where I am fully in charge.

Of course, inspiration and perspiration will work together well. Inspiration strengthens perspiration, but perspiration nurtures inspiration more. We can influence and dance with the Muse, but she usually takes charge of the inspiration. As writers and creators, we are usually 100% in charge of our hard work.

Perspiration is a pain, but we can make it fun by learning and strengthening our creation. It's a lot like exercising — I often have to *make* myself do it.

Perspiration is the hard work of the creative process, including *making time* and *energy* to begin, execute, polish and finish our work.

Other areas of perspiration include dedication, discipline, scheduling, making *zero distractions*, ability to *focus*, organization, making outlines, patience through research, *revisions* and much *polishing*.

Sometimes our perspiration begins before inspiration grabs us. In 1999 I began writing notes *for my own use* wherein I summarized what I understood about depression and mental illness, based on what I had seen in my private practice and what I was reading in clinical literature. After I wrote over half of these 'notes to myself,' I realized that this information was too important not to share with the world. It then took me over 5 years to write my two-volume pair on how repeated trauma caused 'mental illness' as *The Truth about Depression* and *The Truth about Mental Illness*. Most of my usual readers may not know this.

∞ Most of the time, when I, Barbara am starting a new creative endeavor, I have to do a lot of self-talk before I get started. Once I make the commitment to write another book I know I will be taken over by the process and although it is wonderful on one hand, it is *hard work* that completely absorbs me until I finish. I find I need to be alone much of the time, at least in the beginning. There was one time when I knew that I was instantly drafted and that 'fighting' the process was futile. I was lying face down on a massage table when the therapist told me about Cannabis being raised on farms legally. I thought to myself 'Did the farmers know about praying over the seeds and playing soft new age or classical music for the plants? Do people know about the consciousness raising qualities of this plant?' When I got off the table I was already scribbling notes for the book. I threw myself into it and my half of the book was written in 4 months. Most of Charlie and my books take anywhere from a year to five years to finish. The one we did together on *The Power of Humility* took us five years to complete.

Charlie took my cannabis manuscript and then he added his half in 4 months. That book was out in less than a year! We both knew that we were driven by all the years we knew Cannabis was medicine and how we longed to tell our patients how to use it so they could *get off their opiates* and/or *psychiatric drugs*. It was hard work and it was productive. We know we are fortunate to have each other to share in the isolation, percolation, perspiration, inspiration and the joy that comes from being creative. My prayer every time I sit down to write is:

Dear God,
Please help me to get my ego out of the way so you may come through!

Sometimes when I am stuck, I pray:

Help! (one word can be a complete sentence to God!)

(I am not referring to an old man with a long white beard. I am talking to an Intelligence that is bigger and wiser than anything I could begin to imagine but I have faith that it is here, and everywhere. Sometimes it feels like pure love that we are swimming around in.)

And then there is the closing prayer that ends every writing session: Thank you!  ∞

\*     \*     \*

**The Muse** is a key part of our inspiration. She is the goddess of creativity, an otherworldly creature inspiring the artist before and while at work. She has usually been portrayed as a Being who is outside of us. [We believe she is inside of each of us]. Shown on the *next page*, The Muse here gives the poet Hesiod such inspiration by her gentle touch (sometimes called *Shaktipat* within the Kundalini system).

\*     \*     \*

Solitude

In addition to inspiration and perspiration (the hard work of putting together the nuts and bolts of any creative process), we have found that we need four more creative qualities: imagination, freedom, humility and healthy self-care. We address each of these skills in the next chapter.

Hesiod and the Muse, 1891, oil on canvas by Gustave Moreau (no ©)

# 11  The Power of Creativity – *part 2*

→ To use our creative imagination we **need solitude**.

Scientist and inventor *Nikola Tesla* said 'Be alone, that is the secret of invention; be alone, that is when ideas are born.' 'The mind is sharper and keener in seclusion and in uninterrupted solitude.'

This does not mean to be anti-social. It means spend our and your time without distractions from your ideas and stream-of ideas and insights.

Artist and Renaissance man *Walter Russell* said 'Lock yourself up in your room or go out in the woods where you can *be alone*. When you are alone the universe talks to you in flashes of inspiration.'

*Albert Einstein* said 'Be a loner. That gives you time to wonder, to search for the truth.'

The great German writer *Goethe* said 'One can be instructed in society, one is inspired only in solitude. Silence supports discovery in an open mind.'  [Some of these are repeated from above]

# Using Our Imagination

*Imagination* happens when we form ideas, images or sensations outside of our usual ones. It comes from our inborn ability to *invent* these within our mind and our mind's-eye from things outside of our usual world. Using our imagination helps provide meaning to our experience and gives us more understanding to what we already know. It is a basic skill through which we make sense of the world. Our imagination plays a key role as we learn about things new and old.

Most successful inventions and other creative works came from our *imagination*, *inspiration* and *perspiration*. Our creative imaginings are usually effected by our *Set* (mind and mood) and *Setting* (environment). Our imagination can be constructive, destructive or somewhere in between. Depending on the situation, our new ideas may be • healthy/positive/good or • unhealthy/negative/bad.

Some people imagine in a state of tension or gloom to calm them. Others have the effects of repeated childhood or later life traumas and use a lot of negative imagination or worry to defend against their emotional pain, and many suffer unnecessarily. Some, as author Steven King, turn such a curse into a gift and make a living writing about their real or imagined painful experiences. All of this negative imagination or worry drains our Dragon Energy.

The songwriter and trauma survivor John Lennon had a short temper and was often verbally violent with others close to him, yet he wrote a big selling hit song about peace in 'Imagine.'

By contrast, songwriter Justin Hayward did not have a trauma background and used his positive imagination to write and sing some of the most psychologically and spiritually evolved songs ever composed — from 'With the Eyes of a Child' to 'Say It with

Love.' We can use our imagination any way we may wish and commit to doing creatively. It is up to each of us.

Children often use pretend play or stories from their imagination. When children develop fantasy they play at two levels: first, they use role playing to act out what they have developed with their imagination, and at the second level they play again with their make-believe situation by acting as if what they have developed is an actual reality that already exists in narrative myth.

*There is no life I know to compare with pure imagination.*
Willy Wonka

## The Creative Process

We can have a lot of both inspiration and perspiration, and still not write or produce a quality work — one that assists or entertains readers. To write a quality piece, we usually have to be creative. To be creative, we usually have to step outside the box.

Inside the box, we are not usually creative. We are limited in a number of ways: Old beliefs, closed mindedness, political correctness, jargon, rigidity and perfectionism. To get out of the box, we usually do the opposite, as we demonstrate in the attached table. *sections from page 133 through 136,* below and

A single 'aha' experience is not usually enough.

Creativity usually takes at least 5 stages:

1) **Preparation** (focusing on an idea or problem and its dimensions)
2) **Incubation** (we internalize the idea or problem into our unconscious, while externally nothing may appear to be happening)
3) **Intimation** (we get the sense that a solution is on its way)

4) **Illumination** (the creative idea bursts forth into our conscious awareness, as the painting on our cover shows) and finally,

5) **Verification** (the idea is consciously verified, elaborated in writing or other ways, and then applied (from "Art of Thought" by Graham Wallas & Richard Smith, 1926.)

Creativity is not just doing something new or different. We can — and still do — use old, healthy or efficient concepts or principles, but we can now see and use them in expanded ways. With originality, flexibility and time, our creative being expands **outside-the-box** (see pages 135 & 6 for details). This process can take days, weeks, months or years.

### Flow

**Flow** is the feeling experience of energized focus in a task or where we are fully involved, immersed, and successful in the process of the activity. It is an ideal feeling state for us when we are our most creative. Hungarian psychologist Mike Csikszentmihalyi (he says call him Mike) has documented this joyful feeling across several areas of our life.

We are most content or happy when in a flow state—a state of concentration or complete absorption with the activity at hand and the situation. It is an optimal state of intrinsic motivation, where we are fully immersed in what we are doing. This is a feeling everyone has at times, characterized by a feeling of great absorption, engagement, fulfillment, and skill—and during which temporal concerns (time, food, ego-self, and the like) are typically ignored. We are completely involved in an activity for its own sake. The ego falls away. Time flies. The saying 'Time flies when you're having fun' reminds us that being in the flow state is fun—something we trauma survivors may find difficult.* Flow is a completely focused motivation. It is a single-minded immersion in a creative endeavor and represents perhaps the ultimate in harnessing our emotions to perform and learn. In

flow, our feelings are not just focused, but they are pos
energized, and aligned with the task at hand.

> \* **Fun** is the enjoyment of pleasure and, according to Johan Huizinga,
> 'an absolutely primary category of life, familiar to everybody at a
> glance right down to the animal level.' Fun may be encountered in
> many human activities during work, social functions, recreation and
> play, and even seemingly mundane activities of daily living. The
> distinction between enjoyment and fun is difficult to articulate – but
> real, fun being a more *spontaneous, playful,* and *active* event.
>
> Fun is often described as **doing *what you enjoy*,** which can be almost
> any activity imaginable. Including reading about and finding my
> Dragon Energy ?

Common terms for flow include: in the flow, the zone, the
groove, the Now, the Tao, runner's high, the Holy Instant (from
*A Course in Miracles*) or even *Fun*. Historical sources hint that
Michelangelo may have painted the ceiling of the Vatican's
Sistine Chapel while in a flow state: painting for days at a time,
absorbed in his work, not stopping for food or sleep until he
reached the point of passing out. He would awake refreshed
and, upon starting to paint again, re-entered a state of complete
absorption. But most of us don't need to go that long to
experience or appreciate it.

To achieve flow, we match our skill with the challenge of the
task at hand. If the task is too easy or too difficult, flow cannot
occur. Our skill level and challenge level must be matched and
high; if skill and challenge are low and matched, then apathy
results (Figure 11.1 above). The flow state also implies a kind of
focused attention similar to mindfulness, meditation, yoga, and
martial arts which improve our capacity for flow. Among other
benefits, all of these activities train and improve attention. In
short, flow could be described as a state where attention,
motivation, and the situation meet, resulting in a kind of
productive harmony.

Figure 11.1 **Flow** = **Skills vs Challenge** when *Balanced*

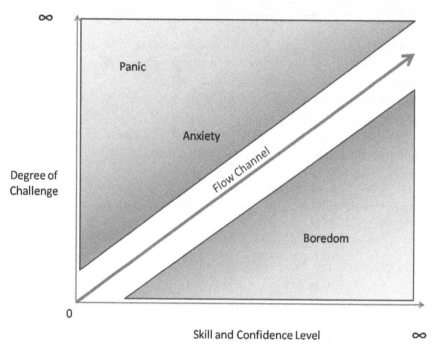

Here are other ways to think about flow:

∞ *Examples* • The stream that comes out of Jet engines has a center called 'the slip.' Around it and what we see from the ground is turbulent. But inside, in the slip it is totally peaceful.

• Inside a hurricane is 'The Eye.' If you've ever experienced a hurricane's eye it is amazing because up until that moment there is extreme turbulence with high winds and a roaring noise. When the eye moves in it becomes completely quiet, no wind, no sound and even bright sunshine.

Take these two examples to give us a 'feeling' quality of how flow can work. Our lives can be busy, even chaotic but when we move into flow and invite creativity to take over, it becomes quiet and peaceful. The turbulence may be all around us — but we are in the slip or the eye and function creatively. And that is also an important feature of Dragon Energy. ∞

### *Ideal Conditions for Flow*

- Clear purpose
- Rapid feedback
- Balanced Challenge and Skill
- No distractions (alone time, in silence)
- No worry or failure
- ego absent
- Autotelic (task is an end in itself)
- Time sense slowed
- Remain in the *Now*
- Action and Awareness merge.

Mike C said 'The best moments in our lives are not the passive, receptive, relaxing times... The best moments usually occur if a person's body or mind is stretched to its limits in a voluntary effort to accomplish something difficult and worthwhile.'

### Be ~ Here ~ Now

For seekers of truth and peace The Eternal Now has been a goal and serious discussion topic for millennia.

*Simple example:* You are **Here** in the **Eternal Now** at the *intersection* of the past (which is gone) and the future (which does not yet exist). Picture your *location in time* where you are always — as you are in the Now — graphically — as a dot.

**You are Currently Here**

This is the single dot • at the intersection of this Infinity sign. This is where you are — right now — which is the only place in time where you can ever be.

With your pen draw a good tiny dot there as shown.

There is **nowhere else** that you can be.

How can we remember this truth? Here are some sources that can help us *Be Here Now* → which will also raise our Dragon Energy in Table 11.1.

How can I change the future? I can't. I can stay Here — Now.

But I have a few choices that we outline below.

Table 11.1 **Paths to *Letting Go* of** [Needing to be in] Control *by **Living Now***

| Working Recovery Aids | Key Terms | Comments |
|---|---|---|
| 1 Twelve Steps of AA & other fellowships | Let go [of ego], and let God | To work the Steps it usually helps to be in the Now, & let go/surrender |
| 2 Generic Spirituality | Eternal Now | From the perennial philosophy that is part of, yet transcends, world religions |
| 3 *A Course in Miracles* | Holy Instant | Sophisticated and effective handbook on ego psychology. Teaches simple prayer as a way out of conflict. Be at peace Now. |
| 4 Ram Dass' teachings | Be Here Now | The 'truth' in this three-word title of his 1971 book |
| 5 Eckhard Tolle teachings | The Power of Now | Let go of ego/false self into the power and peace of Now |
| 6 Power of Humility book by authors | How *Now* fits with **humility** | Teaches how to use humility in relationships Now |

Remember — **For a more positive 'past' and 'future'**

➔ use *these simple actions*

↓

➔ For *Future* **concerns**

➔ use **Anticipation** as a creative strength

➔ For *Past* **concerns**,

➔ use **Grief work with self,  safe**

**others and God**

— see chapters 14 and 15

**Following these simple actions saves each of us**
**a lot of anxiety and worry.**

**The NOW is all that I and we will ever have.**

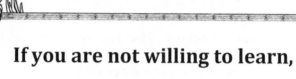

If you are not willing to learn,

no one can help you.

If you determined to learn,

no one can stop you.

Anonymous

# 12   The Power of **Synchronicity**

## Coincidence to → Synchronicity to → Healing

How do each of these differ?

*Coincidence* is a connection between different events occurring closely in time or in space.   Connections can imply principles and possibilities by which to understand the *past*, to inhabit the *present* and to predict the *future*. Beitman

Coincidences are more likely to occur when we **are on the phone, online, doing unusual things, creative efforts** and when we are **upset** or **emotional.**

*Emotional intensity* is increased by births and deaths, marriage and divorce, severe sickness, moving, job changes, vacations and travel, psychotherapy, and apparently unsolvable personal problems.   Major transitions tear the web of our habitual patterns, increasing the possibility that something weird can enter our reality. Beitman

'There's no such thing as a coincidence.
Notice how every major event in your life
somehow leads up to the next
... it's all connected.'
– Unknown creative

**Synchronicity**   Have you ever wondered why — when *two* things happened in your life *occurred* close *together* — that their juxtaposition in time and/or space could have had some kind of *meaning* for you? We can call some of these experiences a *synchronicity*.

A **synchronicity** is a *meaningful coincidence*. When we identify one as occurring for us, a synchronicity can become a pivotal or *growth point*.   But to find one we have to *know what* a synchronicity *is* and have an active and *creative imagination* — both of which are key parts of healthy Dragon Energy. Identifying meaningful coincidences depends upon our attentive mind. What do its 3 parts mean?

---

**Syn** is a prefix meaning *together, joined*-with, *and united.*
**Chron** refers to *time, sequence-in* time, *sequential* or *in order.*
**-Icity** refers to how the prefix and body *terms are related.*

---

When 2 events or experiences *occur* close *together,* we can begin to look for any possible or *potential meanings.* But we do *not* look for whether they *caused* each other. The 2 events or experiences are 'acausal'. While not causing each other, they may have *several* meanings for us.

We simply look for *any association* that could lead to any similarity or connection. Synchronicities are natural, *spontaneous* and *unplanned,* and *natural.* (These are similar to how we created Dragons — also *spontaneous* and *unplanned,* and *naturally.* But as we have described, we made Dragons *over the millennia.*)

*Note:* **Serendipity** *is different and can be confused with it. It means an unplanned, fortunate discovery and Serendipity is a common occurrence throughout the history of product invention and scientific discovery.*

*Synchronicities* usually happen within the same time period — as each half happening within hours to days of the other event or experience.

Psychotherapist and author David Richo PhD said 'Meaningful coincidences and surprising connections occur all the time in our daily lives, yet we often fail to appreciate how they can *guide* us, *warn* us, and *confirm* us on our life's path. Synchronicity is a term first used by Carl Jung to describe coincidences that are *related by* meaningful-ness rather than by cause and effect. These coincidences are life-affecting and yet beyond our control. Jung saw meaningful coincidence, rather than random chance, as a governing dynamic for all of human experience and history. Thus synchronicity underlies our collective as well as our personal destiny.'

Richo continues 'Synchronicity indicates that the timing of events is tied into an unseen pattern of connections. Personally, synchronicity can point us to new challenges or teach us what we need to know.'

### Their Meanings may have Various Levels

→ It all happens in our **mind**. *My* mind. And *yours*, for you.

→ Everything happens here, in our mind. *A Course in Miracles*

Synchronicity is a puzzle we can solve in our Mind. Making meaning from one usually moves us to answers, insight and growth. There is an endless spectrum across which their meanings and their directions can span. Richo gives a simple example: 'On a personal level, Norma orders a red dress for a party but a black dress is delivered to her. As she is about to phone the store to report the error, her sister calls: "Mother has died. Come for the funeral." Norma thought she was in control of her life; she thought she knew what would happen next and what she would need. The synchronous event told her otherwise and outfitted her for what was actually coming next; something much more momentous was about to occur. Synchronicity is the *surprise* that something unplanned or unwanted suddenly fits.'

Table 12.1 **Synchronicity Example Spectrum of Meanings**

| Simple | More Meanings | More Directions | Advanced Meanings |
|--------|---------------|-----------------|-------------------|
| 'Norma's dress' | Attention helps | Imagining helps more | See author examples |
| → Is it the Universe saying you are getting warmer? | | | |

Synchronicity can also work directly or symbolically in a dream, intuition, or premonition. One may speak to an existing situation in our life — and the other 'coincidence' help give us a useful meaning to it. Synchronicity can occur in a dream that reveals what is already true or about to become true. President Lincoln dreamed he would be assassinated one week before the tragedy.

Sudden insights, intuitions or moments of truth are synchronous because they represent explicating moments in which a deeper meaning of our life becomes visible. The function of intuition is to reveal the vast field of possibility in this one moment of insight. 'Gut reactions', intuition, is thus a catalyst to releasing our creativity. *sometimes called*

Conclusion: In any synchronicity we can use the *juxtaposition* and the creative dynamic connection of the 2 experiences to make something meaningful, positive or creative.

### Dragons, Synchronicities and Magic

∞ At the last Dragon Con in 2018 we were sitting around the table in the side room where we had a lot of discussions on Dragon Energy. Over that time Ciruelo had started us on this important topic of 'Dragons, Synchronicities and Magic.' At one point he said — 'When I paint Dragons I get a sense that they are trying to make us aware that we have the ability to experience synchronicities.'

Later he added — 'In my decades-long of painting and studying them, I believe that Dragons are primarily magicians and their message to us is that we are magicians too.' *     ∞

## Dragons and Magic

→ So here we will have to 'shift gears' — so to speak.

'*Magic*' here is a *metaphor* for

## *Taking responsibility* for

## making our individual *life go better*,

which we describe throughout this book. So let's start with a few important 'negative' considerations.

**What this magic is *not*:** Both Dragon magic and our human magic are *not* the sleight-of-hand or 'black magic' that most magicians traditionally perform. Instead, Dragon magic here (*and* the magic of *hermeneutics* and Alchemy — which is the ancient rational science of **interpreting terms within a specific context of being** which **names things accurately** — as we describe in the **third Veil** and the **Portal** of **4 D living**). The Dragon magic within Dragon Energy has three key parts:

*First*, Dragon Energy has its base as *Realness*, which means that we have the natural ability to **be Real** and relate to others from and as our Real Self. *Example* - In mythology, when a magician wants to work magic, he puts a circle around himself which protects him from the threatening dark negative ego character shown in the figure below (Figure 12.1). It is within this bounded circle, this hermetically sealed-off area, that healthy Dragon Energy powers can be brought into play (which are otherwise lost outside the circle, especially if there could be a threatening figure lurking nearby). *This particular circle* represents a *healthy* relationship *boundary*, which I (CW) wrote about in my 1993 book *Boundaries and Relationships*.

**Second**, Dragon magic also means that we each have the ability to move from lower to higher overall psycho-spiritual **vibrations** and thereby *voluntarily raise* our level of awareness and consciousness. By vibrations we are not referring to an ordinary physical kind of vibration where oscillations occur about an equilibrium point, such as in the motion of a tuning fork, the reed in a woodwind instrument, a mobile phone alert or the

Figure 12.1 **The Magician as a Metaphor for the Real or Self-Actualized Person**

(from *Phantasmaphile* April, 2012)

cone of a loudspeaker. Instead, these Dragon magic vibrations are about our *higher energy* and *focus abilities* and our healthy and healing *personal practices* each of us can do *every day*.

add read...

Stretch angled

Examples of ways we can *raise* our *vibrations* are through prayer, meditation, psycho-spiritual contemplation, exercise, yoga, practicing honesty (being Real), optimism and *using our creative imagination* and more. Brian Wilson's 1971 Beach Boys hit song *Good Vibrations* gave us some simple musical hints.

We can usually know that we have reached our goal of having good vibrations when we feel *peace most of the time.*

(number A)

See David Hawkins MD, PhD psychiatrist, physician and developer of a map of consciousness below (Table 12.2). The map's *Log* column is a measure of Hawkins' estimate of vibrations associated with each of his corresponding levels and life views. We say more about them below.

***Third***, to explore Dragon Magic takes another component of Dragon Energy — ***Thinking outside the box***. To develop a quality endeavor, we usually have to be creative. To be creative, we usually have to step outside the box. To do that we *use* our creative imagination.

Inside the box, we are not usually creative. We are limited in a number of ways: Old beliefs, closed mindedness, political correctness, jargon, rigidity and perfectionism. These are traits of Co-dependence, which is a long recurring focus on others to our detriment. To get out of the box, we usually do the opposite of our usual actions, as we demonstrate in the attached table 12.3 and Figure 12.2

Creativity is *not* just doing something new or different. We can — and still do — use old, healthy or efficient concepts or principles, but we can now see and use them in expanded ways.

## Table 12.2 **Map of Consciousness** – via 6 Aspects *

(from David Hawkins)

| MAP OF CONSCIOUSNESS | | | | | |
|---|---|---|---|---|---|
| God-view | Life-view | Level | Log | Emotion | Process |
| Self | Is | Enlightenment | 700 1000 | Ineffable | Pure Consciousness |
| All-Being | Perfect | Peace | ↑ 600 | Bliss | Illumination |
| One | Complete | Joy | ↑ 540 | Serenity | Transfiguration |
| Loving | Benign | Love | ↑ 500 | Reverence | Revelation |
| Wise | Meaningful | Reason | ↑ 400 | Understanding | Abstraction |
| Merciful | Harmonious | Acceptance | ↑ 350 | Forgiveness | Transcendence |
| Inspiring | Hopeful | Willingness | ↑ 310 | Optimism | Intention |
| Enabling | Satisfactory | Neutrality | ↑ 250 | Trust | Release |
| Permitting | Feasible | Courage | ↓ 200 | Affirmation | Empowerment |
| Indifferent | Demanding | Pride | ↓ 175 | Scorn | Inflation |
| Vengeful | Antagonistic | Anger | ↓ 150 | Hate | Aggression |
| Denying | Disappointing | Desire | ↓ 125 | Craving | Enslavement |
| Punitive | Frightening | Fear | ↓ 100 | Anxiety | Withdrawal |
| Disdainful | Tragic | Grief | ↓ 75 | Regret | Despondency |
| Condemning | Hopeless | Apathy | ↓ 50 | Despair | Abdication |
| Vindictive | Evil | Guilt | ↓ 30 | Blame | Destruction |
| Despising | Miserable | Shame | 20 | Humiliation | Elimination |

*These Levels of Consciousness parallel the other psycho-spiritual levels — as in the Chakra system, the Perennial Philosophy, the Twelve Steps, other spiritual paths — and now within Dragon Energy.

In creative thinking, a single insight or 'aha' experience is not usually enough. Dragon Energy Creativity usually takes 5 stages:

1) **Prepare** (focusing on an idea or problem and its dimensions)

2) **Incubate** (we internalize the idea or problem into our unconscious mind, while externally we may appear to be idle while nothing is happening).

3) **Consider, Explore, Intimate** (consider, explore possibilities; we get the sense that a solution is on its way)

4) **Illuminate** (the creative idea bursts forth into our conscious awareness, as the painting on our cover shows). And finally we

5) **Verify** (the idea is consciously verified, elaborated in writing or other ways, and then applied (from "Art of Thought" by Graham Wallas & Richard Smith, 1926.)

With originality, flexibility and time, our creative being expands outside the box. This process can take days, weeks, months or years. We alone decide how fast to move on any project and endeavor.

## Table 12.3. Inside vs Out of the Box Thinking

| Inside – the - Box Thinking | Out of the Box → into Creativity |
|---|---|
| Closed mind | Open mind |
| Arrogant | Humble |
| Pretentious | Real |
| ego oriented | Real Self |
| Surface thinking | Below the surface (Alchemy) |
| Rigid | Flexible |
| Anti free speech | Pro free speech |
| Politically correct | Not PC |
| One belief system | Use our Imagination |
| Closed loop thinking | Enjoy outside our comfort zone |
| Limited word use | Unlimited |
| Limit choices | Consider all choices |
| Fear risk | Careful risk taking |
| Jargon | Rational |
| Perfectionistic | Willing to consider new ideas |
| Ordinary | Extraordinary |
| Judgmental | Non-judgmental |
| Can't tolerate conflict | Tolerate & solve conflict |

Figure **12.2** **Inside & Outside the Box Thinking & Acting**

### ● *Closed Loop Thinking* *

*Theory*     Prior product helps some     *Belief*

Made up, but                                             Theory acceptable

not practical                                             No change needed

Clear disadvantages

*Conflicts of interest*

*Closed loop thinking is - Trying to satisfy or please others to our *creative* detriment, related to *Co-dependence,* which is focusing on others to our detriment.

*Made new It explain*

Are all these above ideas too far outside of a conventional, standard or scientific way of thinking for you? They may not be so weird if we consider the various factors at play. These include our physical, mental, emotional and spiritual parts, the elements and functions that make up the inside of our Real Self. When we use all of these within our creative imagination, it can be a natural experience for us whenever we choose to rise above our ordinary level of consciousness to a higher one and *open our awareness* to experiencing it.

∞ Calling our abilities 'supernatural' until now has often made these traits unreachable. In our research (Barbara) on the after-effects of near death experiences we showed that these kinds of creative abilities are natural and that everyone has this gift if they realize there is a possibility and open them self to it. These kinds of psychic ability range from a new understanding of intuition at the least, all the way to psychic abilities such as the otherwise unexplainable shift to non-ordinary consciousness. This can develop as it should in an otherwise healthy and functioning person who knows how to stay grounded most of the time.

When we become aware about the fact that our mental, physical and spiritual experiences are moved by energies — then we start paying more attention to their possible dimensions. Until now we have been living in a 3 dimensional existence. Recently some of us have been open to higher-dimension-awareness and - living. Intuitions and emotions start revealing to us a new scenario of invisible forces acting around us. Synchronicities, then, become present more often because we are starting to be aware of a richer world full of consciousness.

Is it possible that the Universe (or a Higher Power or the God of our understanding), could be sending us various kinds of positive information and healthy ideas? Awakening to the Dragon Energy that is inherent within us makes us more sensitive to any of these gifts through our Synchronicities that the Universe is sending us all the time.

In most ancient cultures, it was normal for people to have a 'dialogue with the universe' meaning that, for example, if somebody needed help to make a decision they would expect a sign from their environment such as the sound of a bird, a lightning bolt, a peculiar stone found on their path or any other strange event that could be taken as an answer from heaven. For them certain coincidences were considered omens to guide their lives. Shamans of the past were able to identify different forces acting around or within themselves.

In our current culture we don't believe in that 'dialogue with the universe' because our materialistic mind doesn't recognize any consciousness out there apart from ours. We tend to see the universe as a group of inert celestial bodies that exist far away from us but for most ancient cultures there is a common consciousness that encompasses everything. So we should face the tough task of redefining what is external to us and what is internal in order to understand synchronicities, for instance. ∞

Magic is to believe and connect with the Source. I have to be ready and focused to hunt the Muse of inspiration when it appears. The artist grows beauty, chases perfection, probes in the abstract and waits for magic as the peasant waits for the rain. 'The world we live in is an illusion, and you are the magician... Don't get lost in the illusion or your own magic!'

## Richness of Synchronicities in their Subjectivity

Synchronicities have a positive richness. However real and significant they can seem, they are also **subjective** (personal, individual, independent). How can we study a phenomenon that exists so fully in the eye of the beholder? The events of a synchronicity can be
• *simultaneous* or *years apart*. They can be
• *strikingly similar*, or one event can merely *seem* like the
• *answer to the other*.
What seems beyond chance to one person can seem random to another. What looks like a clear message from one angle can be interpreted differently from another angle, or be viewed as altogether meaningless. We believe that synchronicities are
• *opportunities* to make our life go better if we
• *name* them as a synchronicity,
• *consider* what possibilities we the experiencer might have,
• *talk about* them with a safe person,
• *meditate on* them, and
• *follow up*, over time, on their *potential meaning*.
Attention to Synchronicities raises our Dragon Energy.

*The mind is powerful.*
*When you filter it with positive thoughts,*
*your life will start to change.*

Gautama Buddha

# 13  *Our* Synchronicities as Examples

Our life *events* and *experiences* are like a hall of doors. When one door closes, another usually opens. Of course, no one can tell us the most important details about what will be behind each door and how to navigate the hallway and each door.

Sometimes we may be standing in that hallway for a long time, waiting on a door to open that might not open. But we often look so long and so regretfully upon the closed door that we do not see the one that has already opened for us.

Below we begin our stories of our personal synchronicities as examples for you the reader to help your navigation of ones that will come up for you in your life. We also have other personal examples in chapters 9, 12, 13 and the *Appendix* on page 199.

101, 127 and 139.

Synchronicities are usually best described through **narratives** or **stories**.
Here below we will give you selected ones of ours.
Some will blend with our other synchronicities in other chapters.

**Barbara meets Ken Ring** — In 1981, I was going through a pile of magazines at a friend's house. In an old *Omni Magazine* one article caught my eye about a professor of Psychology at the University of Connecticut. Kenneth Ring PhD was gathering first hand stories of people who had "died" and returned reporting similar experiences: they

• Left their body and they had

• Been in a tunnel, meeting Guides,

• Seeing the Light,

• A boundary or border that if crossed, they would not be allowed to return,

• Some of them preferring to stay but being sent back anyway, and retaining a

• Sense of peace they brought back.

I wrote him at the University to tell him about the patients who reported this to me while I was attending to their respiratory therapy needs. Ring wrote me back and through his coaxing I told him about my near-death experience (NDE) after back surgery while suspended in the circle bed.

Coincidently — and this became a series of synchronicities — he was going to be speaking at a small Paranormal conference 10 minutes from my house in south Florida. We agreed that I would come to his talk and then we would have lunch.

As I sat in the audience with some 90 people, Ring listed the stages of the near-death experience. I got goose bumps. The night before I had seen the movie 'Resurrection' with Ellen Burstyn. After her NDE she had many changes including the energy arousal that many of us experience. And now, one day later I was sitting and listening to the top researcher in the field of near-death studies reporting on what they had found about coming back from the first stages of the dying process.

Ring ended by asking if anyone in the audience had an NDE and would be willing to share about it. When no one raised their hand, he asked if Barbara Harris was there and I reluctantly raised my hand. I stood because he invited me to share what had happened. Except for one relative, a few nurses and the psychiatrist I saw while I was in the body cast, I had never told anyone my experience. (The nurses had called what I told them a "hallucination." The psychiatrist had suggested psychoanalysis with him 3 or 4 times a week after my cast came off and I finished physical therapy. I did not open that door and never returned to his office.)

As I stood and knew — but was afraid to look — that all eyes were upon me, I told my NDE. When I finished they were silent. After what seemed like an eternity, they loudly applauded. I was embarrassed but relieved as I sat and had lunch with Ken, who—along with the audience minutes before— had validated me.

This was the beginning of my giving talks on NDEs and later my writing several books on them. In a few months I was asked to educate the nursing staff of Mt. Sinai Hospital on South Miami Beach where I had done my clinical respiratory therapy training. At the same time I was published in the *Respiratory Therapy Journal* about the new subject I called "The emotional needs of critical care patients."

A few months later Ring came back to Florida, this time to Palm Beach where he was meeting with a group of possible donors to support his NDE research. I drove there and walked into his hotel. He was slouched in a lounge chair and the minute I saw him said, "You don't look so good. Instead of meeting with me would you like to go up to your room and rest?" He told me he had a terrible headache but there was no time for him to rest because his next meeting was coming up.

After my NDE I had started to have odd after-effects happen that I later found were common. For example, my hands, especially my palms were beginning to feel warm as they had many times while working with a patient who needed to be touched. I asked Ring if I could try putting my hands on his head and neck to see if that would help. "Of course," he said. My right hand settled on the back of his neck and my left was on his forehead. Within minutes he said that his headache was gone and he asked me if I had ever heard the term "Kundalini." I hadn't. He suggested that I look into it and tell him what I thought. I agreed.

The next weekend I found a bookstore and there on a shelf were several books on Kundalini energy. I bought John White's *Kundalini, Evolution and Enlightenment,* and Lee Sanella MDs *Kundalini, Psychosis or Transcendence.*

After reading both books I was convinced that Ken Ring was onto something important. And as one synchronicity led to another and another, I left Respiratory work and was led to researching the aftereffects of these spiritually transformative experiences.

We explain what all this has to do with Dragon Energy throughout this book. But for now it supports how useful being open to recognizing synchronicities in our personal day-to-day life are helpful to enliven us in our inner life and outer life, giving us more Energy.

We continue with **more** of our *Synchronicities* on the next page.

**We meet Ciruelo**. Charlie had earlier been at Dragon Con for 2 years with friends. By his third year (2015) I joined him. The first afternoon a lecture caught my eye by an artist named Ciruelo who's focus was on Dragons as art. I realized later that he was actually *the* honored artist by the convention that year of 2015. One of his paintings was on the cover of the program book. He called it 'Flight Instructors,' who were shown as the 3 fairies guiding the beautiful girl standing atop the Dragon's nose (see painting on Dragon Con Program Book next page.)

He was on the schedule to talk about the history of Dragons world-wide. I decided to go to that one for an intro into the world of the Dragon. The lecture hall was over to the side of the huge art show in the lower exhibits level of the Atlanta Hyatt Regency Hotel. Hundreds of paintings of Dragons, fantasy art and scores of artists in their booths waiting to answer questions or sell their art. These artists were unusual because they were all happy, not just sitting in a booth to sell their wares.

Charlie and I had taught for over 30 years at psychology and trauma recovery conferences. Many survivors of trauma and the therapists who treat them attend. They were and still are serious and sometimes painful conferences. I had also spoken at many NDE-related meetings and conferences for decades.

By contrast, at Dragon Con we experienced a new kind of playfulness. It was and is a serious and playful science fiction and fantasy conference. Part of its lively ambiance was from some 1 in 6 adults dressing in costumes related to Sci-Fi Fantasy, including super heroes. This kind of conference experience contrasted from how so many of us NDErs change in that many of us acquire a deep sensitivity to energies.

So with over 40 years now of this sensitivity to energies it was startling for me to walk into this Sci-Fi and Fantasy convention and its related art show. I wandered for a while through the aisles of booths containing paintings, sculptures and jewelry all dedicated to the images of Dragons, fantasy figures and super heroes and more until it was time for us to hear Ciruelo's lecture.

(For more see my [BW] 1995 book *Spiritual Awakenings:* Insights of the NDE and Other Doorways to Our Soul or my earlier book *Full Circle*).

I am 76 and Charlie is 81. We still love to learn. Besides being authors, therapists and teachers, wherever we were invited to teach, we also attended many of the other speakers' lectures to learn more. We sit in the front row so we can see and hear better, as we did here at Dragon Con too.

Ciruelo walked in and when he started to talk I was taken in by his beautiful Spanish accent. As he went through his slides of Dragons from all over the world, I had a sense of Joseph Campbell's scholarly lectures on how most myths from all over the world were linked, many with the same mythological story although the different cultures hadn't met. Campbell brought the 'Power of Myth' back to the 'Hero's Journey.' Every culture has these stories that describe our journey through life as we become our own Hero.

Ciruelo's lecture that day showed me the mythical Heroes journey through many beliefs and traits in the Dragon. From that moment on, we have been interested in the Dragon myths because they once again reveal what Charlie and I have been teaching – life is about our own growth to become all that God, a Higher Power or the Universe wants for us. What I personally have experienced after my Near-Death Experience over 40 years ago, is that this search takes us to our deepest inner being where we are pure Love. And that Love is the primary characteristic of God. Over the past 5 years we have found that one of many paths on Earth to this journey of awakening is through Dragon Energy.

There are Dragons everywhere in most cultures, past and present. There are 'bad' dragons that destroy and there are 'good' dragons that are Heroes. Ciruelo's slides that first day were breathtaking for us, including when he showed pictures of the celebrations that his village in Spain holds yearly to celebrate the Dragon.

Please understand that we who have opened or awakened to levels of consciousness beyond the normal every day ho-hum existence – fall in love easily and I did that day with Ciruelo's great understanding of the Dragon. I thought that if his energy is that of a Dragon – then Dragons must have a beautiful side that most artists don't show. Ciruelo does. His dragon paintings contain many aspects of the "Hero's Journey."

We went to Ciruelo's booth and met Daniela, Ciruelo's wife and she showed us more of his work in books he had written about the Dragons and other books that he had illustrated. We stood in that booth for the rest of the afternoon asking questions and constantly smiling over the joy we had found.

That evening we had dinner with the Cabral's including their two delightful teenagers, Angelo and Lys. By the end of Dragon Con 2015 we were invited to the fabulous suite Dragon Con had given the Cabrals because Ciruelo was the featured artist that year. We spent time with them the day after Dragon Con was over. And we all hugged good-bye and wished each other everything good until we would see them next year.

**2016** The best part of the 2016 Dragon Con was that Ciruelo brought his family almost a week early and stayed with us. We showed them Atlanta early before the conference. The differences between our two cultures gave us much to talk and laugh about. What amazed me the most was how well this family relates to each other.

**2017** Highlights of 2017, having dinner every evening with Ciruelo, Daniela, Angelo and Lys. Sometimes my son and his family would join us. The other highlights include, 7 line dancing dinosaurs at 3 in the morning, dancing in the lobby. We were on the $22^{nd}$ floor of the Atrium at the Hyatt and could hear them (They made such a ruckus that many of us were out on the

balconies watching and laughing. There was also
wrestling and BattleBots to add to the humor. (By the way,
that we have requested the International Tower because there
is no atrium and it is quieter – sort of!)

Needless to say, I am proud of my family and the way they
have raised their children. But spending time with Ciruelo,
Daniela, Angelo and Lys in a relaxed manner, walking around
Piedmont Park and just hanging out, I saw how healthy they all
are. And now, 4 years into being together, I know we are
family. The love among us is beautiful, joyful and full of an
Energy that we are going to [try to] describe in this book.

**2018** Finally, this Dragon Con I was thrilled to buy this painting
from Ciruelo. When I look at it – it takes me back to my
moment when I left my old life and with fear jumped into my
new life. I look at this painting now every day and it brings back
what I learned when I jumped. I learned what real courage is.
We feel the fear and we do it anyway. Those faeries and that
gentle Dragon were with me the whole time. It was not the
frenetic energy of fear that drove with me those 16 days. It was
the Dragon Energy that pushed me (while the faeries pulled)
even though I was fearful. I look at the dragon in this painting
and I gratefully thank it for being with me. Dragon Energy is
mainly ineffable but it is also almost palpable.

If we ignore or are numb to our fear – and do something
anyway -- that is insanity. However, and here is an important
trait of Dragon Energy. If we are afraid or scared and — with
courage — do it anyway with full knowledge of our fear – that is
Dragon Energy. Identifying with the Dragon in this way gives
us *courage*.

We have had numerous talks with Ciruelo about Dragons and
their lore now into 5 years. Long ago at a workshop, we were
asked to write down what we would like to be written on our

headstone when we die. I wrote 'She learned how to risk, and indeed she did.' That is Dragon Energy.

We look forward to experiencing more meaningful coincidences now at Dragon Con 2019. There we will be panel speakers with Ciruelo in 3 sessions set in Dragon Con's wonderful Art Department.

For several more personal synchronicities stories as examples see chapters 4, 9 and 12.

This chapter on **Naming** Traumas Correctly

+ the next one on **Healing** from Trauma Effects

may contain the most powerful and important

information in this book.

It could help you craft a better life

# 14  The Power of *Naming* Traumas Correctly

## ... **is Healing** *and* **Raises Dragon Energy**

**Trauma** is a fact of life. Living an enjoyable and long life on this planet is not easy. We are often stressed — not by just the earthly elements outside of us such as bad weather and the like — but *most often* by *other people* stressing and hurting us in different ways.

Most of us are trauma survivors and most of us don't know it. All of our **school systems** — *K through high school, through graduate school* **still don't teach** what trauma **is** or how to handle and treat it. It took researchers and health professionals a long time — until the early 1980s simply to name it as *Post-Traumatic Stress Disorder* (PTSD). Even so, we had known for millennia (*thousands of years*) that repeated trauma existed — but we didn't know how to recognize, figure out, de-cipher and frame its results on us — the survivors.

### What is Trauma?

Trauma occurs when any act, event or experience harms or damages any one or more of our *physical*, sexual, *mental*, emotional or *spiritual* integrity that resides within the sanctity of our True Self.

*Other terms* for **True Self** include: Real Self, Child Within, Inner Child, Divine Child, and Higher Self. It has also been called our Deepest Self, our Inner Core. These terms each refer to the *same core* and center that is in us — as us. It is who we are when we feel most authentic, genuine or spirited *and more*. See page 108 for a summary of the many terms for our True Identity. (We capitalize the terms' first letters to show its *importance for us in living* and to *help differentiate* it *from* the *false* or *lower self*, which is our *ego*.)

## Trauma Drains Our Energy

Experiencing hurts, losses and traumas drains and lowers our Energy. It drains and lowers our Dragon Energy. *Recognizing* and **naming** these traumas and finding out how to heal from them will likely renew and *increase* our Dragon Energy. In this and the next chapter we will describe how to begin to do that.

**Who are the perpetrators** of these traumas? We shouldn't be paranoid, but abusers, neglecters and all who inflict any traumas could be anyone. Among the most common people who mistreat, abuse or neglect us are our *own family* members and especially our *parents* or *parent figures* (most of whom are *themselves unknowing* trauma survivors). Our siblings, at times, may also mistreat or abuse us.

Also — outside of our family our *peers* in *school* and *neighborhood* can abuse us. Less commonly a stranger can abuse us. Some come *online* and abuse or bully us. The key in all of these is to **recognize** each trauma when it happens and then **name** it *when it happens* and then share it with a safe person (see page 157) or write it down in a safe place such as our journal or diary. and 166

No one knows how many or what percentage of people grow up with a healthy amount and quality of love, guidance and other nurturing. We can estimate it. From my 40 years of experience working in the trauma and healing field I (CW) estimate that perhaps 5 to 20% of us had healthy parenting. This means that from 80 to 95% of people did not receive the love, guidance and other nurturing necessary to form consistently healthy relationships, and to feel good about themselves and about what they do in life.

So — most families across the world are dysfunctional in that they don't provide and support the healthy needs of their children. What results is an *interruption* in the otherwise normal and *healthy neurological* and *psychological growth* and *development* of the child from *birth to adulthood*.

Please look carefully at Figure 14.1 from the **ACE study** below and discussions on pages 202 and 205. For one of several websites and descriptions of the ACE Study practical meanings see theannainstitute.org slides presentations.

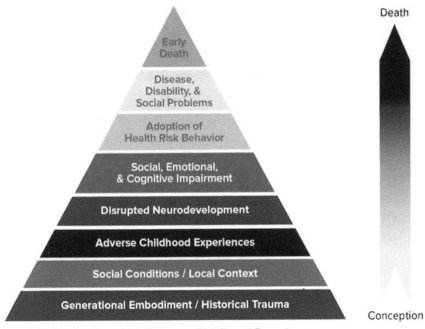

Mechanism by which Adverse Childhood Experiences
Influence Health and Well-being Throughout the Lifespan

## We are Survivors

To survive, the traumatized child's Real Self (True Self/Child Within) **goes into hiding** deep within the unconscious part of its psyche. What emerges is a *false self* or ego which tries to run the show of our life, but is unable to succeed because our ego is simply a defense mechanism against pain and not real (we introduced this on our mind and ego description in the *Introduction*). The ego's motives are based mostly — if not nearly always — on *needing to be right* and *in control*. The following pencil drawing came from a savvy trauma survivor who attended a talk to some 150 people that I gave on trauma and healing decades ago.

When a child grows up in a crazy (abusive, traumatic, or neglectful) family and a traumatic and sometimes crazy world, several crucial things happen. Their associated emotional pain becomes so intense that the child's Real Self goes into hiding (Figure 14.2 below). To survive, the traumatized child over-develops a false self (ego), and as part of the process it learns to use several mechanisms and dynamics to defend itself from the inordinate emotional pain that it experiences repeatedly. We can summarize and describe a large part of these *defense mechanisms* most simply as involving and often being Core Issues, described below.

Note the half-smiling face atop the figure that represents the false self, which is the ego. The dark globules or dots surrounding the Child represent the negative messages (threats, guilts, shames) from our *parents* and parent figures *and peers*. 'You are bad, you did bad, and the like.' When these usually *untruths* are regularly repeated, they not only drain and lessen our otherwise healthy God-given energy and make us vulnerable to sickness (physical or mental-emotional illness), but they often become painful *Core Issues* in living and healing.

## Figure 14.2 The Child (Real Self) Goes into Hiding

*messages from impactful relationships "The Split"*

# The 15 Core Issues

Repeated early life stresses and traumas have a negative effect on brain structure and function. These increase the risk of ongoing life problems with our relationship with our self and others.

An **issue** is any conflict, concern or potential problem, whether conscious or unconscious, that is incomplete for us or needs action or change. A ***core* issue** is one that *comes up repeatedly*.

There are at least 15 common core issues in relationships, recovery and life that we can recognize, name and work through. These include:

## The Core Issues

- **Control** (Needing to be in Control)
- **Trust** (Difficulty Trusting)
- **Being Real** (Difficulty being Real)
- **Feelings** (Difficulty handling Feelings)
- **Low self-esteem** (Shame, not good enough))
- **Dependence** (over dependent or over-focusing on others)
- **Fear of abandonment**
- **All-or-none** thinking and behaving
- **High tolerance** for inappropriate behavior
- **Over-responsibility for others**
- **Neglecting** my **own needs**
- **Grieving** my un-grieved losses
- **Difficulty resolving conflict**
- Difficulty **giving love,** and difficulty **receiving love**

At first it may not be clear just which one or perhaps more of these core issues may be involved for us. Core issues do not usually present themselves to us as an 'issue.' Rather, they present at first as problems in our everyday living.

When these painful patterns come up for us, we can share then with selected safe and supportive people. As we persistently consider and tell our story to safe others it will generally become clear just which issue or issues are involved. This knowledge will be helpful in our gradually getting free of our associated confusion, discontent, and unconscious negative life patterns (repetition compulsions or re-enactments).

**Naming** the issue, i.e., giving it an accurate name, **Demystifies** (which means to make something clear and easy to understand, to explain something so that it no longer confuses or mystifies someone) the otherwise everyday problem and opens us to processing and ultimately healing from its previously nagging emotional pain. Naming gives us personal power, takes us through the portal of 4 Dimensional living (see Special Section) and increases our Dragon Energy.

## The New Hidden Traumas

Since the 1980s a new trauma category and group has emerged that has been carefully hidden by the drug industry (Big Pharma) and by most of the organized medical professions. And it will be essentially as important to name them correctly as we do the above traumas. These include the large sub-group of chemicals known as **psychiatric drugs**.

After decades of research and publishing books and articles on the topic, I was invited by the journal's editors to write an article on this topic which was published in the *International Journal of Risk & Safety in Medicine* in 2010 which I titled as **Psychiatric Drugs as agents of Trauma**. These drug classes include antidepressants, antipsychotics, mood stabilizers and benzodiazepines. Their mechanism of action is not healthy. They act by *intoxication* and *disabling the brain*. Here is my briefest summary (the full article is available free by an online search).

Drawing on the work of numerous psychiatrists and psycho-pharmacologists* and my own observations, I describe how most ᴎ psychiatric drugs are not only toxic but can be *chronically* ⁱc, which I define in some detail throughout this paper. In to observing this occurrence among numerous of my patients over the past 20 years, I surveyed 9 mental health clinicians who had taken antidepressant drugs long-term. Of these 9, 7 (77%) experienced bothersome toxic drug effects and 2 (22%) had become clearly worse than they were before they had started the drugs. Based on others' and my observations I describe the genesis of this worsened condition which I call the *Drug Stress Trauma Syndrome*. (Over the last 9 years I continued to see countless more with this syndrome.)

These toxic drug effects can be and are often so detrimental to the users' quality of life among a significant minority of patients that they can no longer be considered trivial or unimportant. Instead, they are so disruptive to many patients' quality of life that their effect becomes traumatic, and are thereby agents of trauma. These observations and preliminary data may encourage others to look into this matter in more depth.

*Examples of these experts include: Leo Hollister MD, PhD, Peter Breggin MD, David Healy MD, RJ Baldessarini MD, Gail Jackson MD, Joanna Moncrieff MD, Sami Timimi MD and Robert Whitaker. These are the tip of the 'Iceberg'. [handwritten: Names ... 8 observers & expert]

If any reader may want to stop any of these drugs I advise that they do so *slowly* over weeks to months under a doctor's care. For help, see my book *Not Crazy*: You May Not be Mentally Ill. A final trauma often used by many psychiatrists includes Electric Shock Treatment (ECT), which Peter Breggin and others have long described (see References and Breggin's Youtubes).

## *Private* Trauma Self-Checks

We include 2 trauma surveys for any reader who may be interested in doing a *private* self-assessment as to whether you may have experienced traumas at any time in your life in the Appendix on pages 202 and 205. No other person will see your results unless they open your book to that page. → In the next chapter we show how to heal from the ongoing pain of these trauma effects.

# 15     The Power of

# Healing from Traumas

The tried-and-true ways to begin healing from these and other trauma effects is to focus on several tasks, which I described in my books over 30 years ago (*Healing the Child Within* in 1987 and its workbook *A Gift to Myself* in 1990). Their principles and actions remain tested and validated by trauma specialists today worldwide.

To rediscover our *True* or *Real Self* and heal our *Child Within* (all terms for our *True Identity*) i.e., lessen our mental, emotional, and physical and relationship-related pain, we can begin a process that involves the following four **actions** that are also Core Issues.

## The 4 Healing Actions

• Discover and practice being our **Real Self** or *Child Within*. (Being Real is the most powerful action we can do to heal from trauma pain and eventually make our life go better.)

• Identify our ongoing physical, mental-emotional and spiritual **needs**. Practice getting these needs met with safe and supportive people.

• Identify, re-experience and **grieve** the pain of our ungrieved losses or traumas in the presence of safe and supportive people.

• Identify and work through our **Core** recovery **Issues**.

These four actions are closely related. Working on them slowly over time, and thereby healing our hurt Real Self, generally occurs in a circular fashion, with work and discovery in one area often being a link to another area.

*Summary*: **All 4 Actions Raise our Dragon Energy**

→ Be **Real**.

→ Find **Need**s.

→ **Grieve** our unhealed Traumas.

→ Find and work **Core Issues**

***Naming*** all the parts and sub parts of these actions and our personal experiences **right, correctly** or **accurately** is a *key* to help us heal from our trauma effects and self-raise our Energy, which in this book we also call Dragon Energy.

## Setting Healthy Boundaries

To even start doing any of these 4 Actions requires having boundaries. Learning about and setting healthy boundaries is crucial for our survival from birth to death.

We get stuck in all-or-none thinking and behaving when we remain attached to our ego/false self. The false self can make only walls, not healthy boundaries. Walls tend to alienate others, in contrast to assertive healthy boundaries that often work better to get what we want.

**As I begin to live from and as my True Self,**
**I can learn to set healthy boundaries and limits,**
**which in turn will allow me many more choices in my life.**
**With this new insight and understanding I can choose among any one or**
**more of the many points along the many spaces across the all-or-none**
**spectrum from zero to ten.**

This is a description of clear-thinking trauma survivors identifying and using advanced Dragon Energy. To do that we have to name things accurately (which is also the base of the second Veil and which is also the portal in 4 D living and eventually to 5 D living and alpha Dragon Energy (see Special Section).

## *The Dragon as Guardian*

In Mythology one legend is that the Dragon *guards* and *protects* the Treasure. On the surface of the myth the 'Treasure' is usually the symbol representation of gold and jewels — and sometimes an innocent maiden. But as is true for many myths and similar systems, what is shown on the surface is *not* its *real meaning*.

To find the Real Treasure, we have to *go beneath the surface claim* of 'truth' that anyone can publish. This is a basic principle of science, rationality, sagacity, clear-thinking Dragon Energy, gnosis, Alchemy and wisdom. We have to go outside-the-box and explore other realms — as via our creative imagination and our occasional peeks into the Imaginal Realm that we have discussed several times in this book.

The **Treasure** here is our own True Identity, our Real Self, Child Within, individual Reality, our free consciousness (see also page 108 for the many names we have for it)

*107*

Our ego and other people are the common thief or villain that steals or attacks our Real Self. Our Dragon Energy uses healthy boundaries to guard and protect us.

***Clinical example***: I (CW) had a 28-year-old trauma survivor patient who had post-traumatic stress disorder (PTSD). He had been sexually and emotionally abused by his high school sports coach for months. When he reported the abuse, the school principal did not believe him, did not fire the coach and his parents only reluctantly believed him. He distrusted them all.

In several of my psychotherapy sessions with him he described a credible metaphor to help him heal. The image was of the Heisman trophy (which from 1935 was a special trophy awarded yearly to the NCAA college football player who showed the most outstanding performance with integrity). He said that for him the held and carefully protected *football* represented his Real Self, Child Within (as his 'Treasure') and the *extended arm* was his healthy boundary to keep any abusers away (Figure 15.1).

**Difficulty handling and resolving conflict** is a common core issue, including during all three of these classical recovery stages:

→ now p. 162

### The Stages of Recovery

• **Stage 1** is **Stabilizing** any **basic illness**,

• **Stage 2** is **Trauma healing**,

• **Stage 3** is **Spiritual work**.

Figure 15.1 **The *Heisman* Trophy** (top of)

Over the course of 6 months of weekly psychotherapy he expressed his emotional pain and worked on his core issue of *Difficulty Trusting*. He had also worked on another common core issue: Difficulty Handling and Resolving Conflict, which we summarize below. We use this Core Issue as an *example* of addressing some of the details of one of the 15 listed on page 154 above.

Difficulty handling conflict usually interacts with most of the other core issues. (I [CW] describe these stages of recovery in detail and more in *A Gift to Myself* and *Wisdom to Know the Difference*: Core Issues.)

## Core Issue of Difficulty Handling Conflict

Growing up in a troubled or dysfunctional family — to survive the pain — we learn to *avoid* conflict *whenever* we can. We may have seen our parents and other family members model poor conflict handling and resolution. When conflict occurs, we learn to withdraw from it in some way. Occasionally, we become aggressive and try to overpower and control those with whom we are in conflict. When these actions fail, we may become devious and attempt to manipulate. In a dysfunctional environment, using these methods may help assure our survival. But they do not tend to work for us in a healthy intimate relationship.

Recovery begins by *observing each conflict* as it comes up and then *working through* it. But the fear and other painful feelings that come up as we get closer to the conflict may be too much for us to tolerate or experience. Rather than face the pain and the conflict head-on, we may revert to our prior methods of all-or-none and the like by over-controlling or withdrawing.

In handling and resolving conflict we first *recognize* that we *are in it*. We *name* the issue as that we are *in conflict* about and that we may need to go within and share our story with safe others and *explore how* to resolve it. We then take a risk if we feel safe, to disclose our concerns, feelings, wants and needs.

It is nearly always useful *not* to scream or yell at the other(s) with which we may be in conflict, since doing so usually escalates and elevates the conflict to un-resolvable levels. (Screaming or yelling also drains our own and close others' Dragon Energy.) By working through conflict, we gradually learn to identify and work through our past conflicts and current ones as they come up for us. It takes courage to recognize and to work through conflict.

## Choices in Handling Conflicts

Before recovery, many of us may have used an all-or-none approach to handle our conflicts. We fight or attack the other party. Or we may run away, withdraw, hide or decline to engage them in working through our differences. While some minor conflicts may be appropriately and successfully mostly ignored (see lower 2 rows of Table 15.1), the most efficient approach is usually to face it head-on, engage the other party as needed and work it through.

Depending on with whom we may be in conflict, we usually have several choices regarding which problem-solving tools or skills we can enlist. For a general or generic approach to resolve a conflict, consider using a problem-solving approach as we outline in Tables 15.1 and 15.2 below.

**Table 15.1 Levels, Consequences and Attention needed to help Solve Conflicts** (see *Wisdom to Know the Difference*: *Core Issues* for details)

| Level | Threats of loss and Consequences | Attention* | Possible Lessons Learned |
|-------|----------------------------------|------------|--------------------------|
| 5 | Life threatening | Total focus required | • Sort out or prioritize each conflict's seriousness. |
| 4 | **Major** loss *probable* | Near total focus | • If a low threat, identify & address any of the triggering factors |
| 3 | Major loss *possible*, but unlikely | More as needed to prevent the loss | • If a low threat, identify & address any of the triggering factors |
| 2 | **Minor** loss *probable* | Some as needed | • Use a combined mental & spiritual approach to resolve conflict. |
| 1 | Minor loss *possible*, but unlikely | Little | • Use a combined mental & spiritual approach to resolve conflict. |
| 0 | Inconsequential | Little or none | • Remember & repeat the Serenity Prayer when need. |

*For all conflict levels, *gathering **more information*** usually helps resolve it.

# ls of Conflict and Ways to Handle or Resolve

How much focus you devote to your plan and how much action you take will determine how likely you will be to resolve your conflict. The 7 main *adversaries* in conflict are:

**The Person** (i.e., **US**) vs:
1) Our *Self* (internal conflict), vs.
2) *Another Person*,
3) *Society/world*,
4) *Nature*,
5) *Technology*,
6) '*God*,' and
7) '*Fate*.'

We show our choices in **resolving** a conflict in Table 15.2 below (originally from page 95 of my book Wisdom to Know the Difference: *Core Issues* in Relationships and Living).

### Table 15.2 Possible Methods and Solutions to Handling Conflicts

| Possible Solutions | Description & Comments |
|---|---|
| 1. **Fight** | Attack the other party verbally |
| 2. **Flight** (Run away**) or Freeze** | Withdraw, hide, and decline engaging in working it through. |
| 3. **Engage the conflict & work it through** | Usually the most productive. Can use a general approach or consider 4 other ways as shown below. |
| • **Fair Fighting** | Developed decades ago for couples who tend to fight unfairly. |
| • **Approach by Spiritual Levels (with Humility)** | Understanding the usual conflict in triangles, this allows new and higher ways to solve many conflicts. See p X |
| • **ego detachment** | As described in teachings from AA/Al-Anon to *A Course in Miracles* |
| • **Admit powerless over _____** | As in Step One of the Twelve Steps; use Serenity Prayer |

Working through our cycles of healing as described above in the Hero's Journey chapters 3 and 4, we tell our story to safe people *or 12-step group.*

such as our counselor~ or~ therapist. We begin to identify our
hurts, losses and traumas from our past and grieve them as
they come up. And as core issues surface for us, we talk about
them and work through them. Healing our hurt Real Self does
not usually occur in a linear fashion. Rather, it tends to occur in
waves or in a circular fashion and then in a spiral one, as does
our story. Each time we complete and integrate a story — that
particular 'episode' of our life story, we are then free to create a
newer, bigger and more truthful or honest story. Part of this
truth and honesty has to do with our Being Real. As we progress
and grow in life, we then compile and create bigger and bigger
stories and then integrate each into our life.

Figure 15.2 – **Recovery and Growth through Experiencing,
Telling our Story and Observing it All**

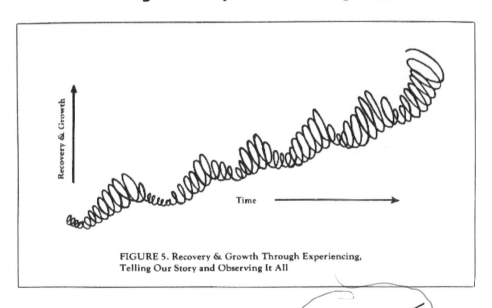

FIGURE 5. Recovery & Growth Through Experiencing,
Telling Our Story and Observing It All

### *Risking* Being Real

*199*

Open to the Appendix Item 1 on page 200 and read the poem.
Give yourself some time to reflect on it. What was it like for you
to read the poem? I may have trusted some people in my past
and they ended up hurting me. So how can I really tell?

My experience is that there is no 100% sure way to tell without experimenting, using trial and error or a share-check-share approach.

**Table 5.3  Some Characteristics of Safe and Unsafe People**

| Safe | Unsafe |
|---|---|
| ➤ Listen to you | ➤ Don't listen |
| ➤ Hear you | ➤ Don't hear |
| ➤ Make eye contact | ➤ No eye contact |
| ➤ Accept the real you | ➤ Reject the real you |
| ➤ Validate the real you | ➤ Invalidate the real you |
| ➤ Non-judgmental | ➤ Judgmental |
| ➤ Are real with you | ➤ False with you |
| ➤ Clear | ➤ Unclear |
| ➤ Boundaries appropriate and clear | ➤ Boundaries unclear, messages mixed |
| ➤ Direct | ➤ Indirect |
| ➤ No triangles | ➤ Triangle-in others |
| ➤ Supportive | ➤ Competitive |
| ➤ Loyal | ➤ Betray |
| ➤ Relationship authentic | ➤ Relationship feels contrived |

from p 47 Core Issues book

To risk being real with people takes *courage, motivation, awareness* and the *discernment* to seek out and find *safe* others. To do that is not always easy. It takes practice and trial and error. On the next page I list some key characteristics of safe people compared to unsafe ones. Look this over carefully.

Not all of these safe/unsafe characteristics are absolute. For example, some people who make eye contact, appear to listen to you and are at times supportive may *still* be unsafe. And a safe person may be unclear at times. But, over time, these characteristics may be helpful in differentiating who is safe from who is unsafe.

Have you *met* anyone who feels safe to you?

Do you *know* anyone *now* who feels safe?

Has it been scary or difficult for you to find safe people?

If you have a few minutes, reflect on who you knew in the past and who you know now. Include anyone who comes up in your awareness. Of these people, who has felt safe—or *feels* safe to you now. In the space below write in either the names, initials, description or a code word for anyone who felt or feels safe to you now. Remember, this is your private journal, so what you write in it is for your eyes only.

_____

_____

_____

Next, list any *un*safe people in your life in the space below. Take your time doing these experiential exercises. When you come to a point where you feel that you've about completed your list of safe people, consider the following. Pick one person on the list, perhaps the safest. Meet with them in person and tell them how and why you feel safe with them (if they are too far away, you might consider calling them.)

_____

_____

_____

What was this like to do this exercise? What was it like to share what you did with your safest person? What feelings came up or are coming up for you now? In the space below write your answers to these questions, and/or write whatever is coming up for you right now. Take as much time and space as you need.

_____

_____

_____

_____

_____

_____

_____

_____

For my books which have similar exercises within their pages to some degree, see my books *A Gift to Myself* and *Wisdom to Know the Difference: Core Issues in Relationships, Recovery and Living.*

*If alcohol or drugs are involved, see  Not Crazy*: You May Not be Mentally Ill.

# 16      The Power of Love – 1

Love is usually the most psychologically and spiritually invigorating of our feelings. Yet, most of us have been hurt over love by disappointment, rejection and betrayal. As a result we often become reluctant to risk expressing our love to anyone. And we may not trust others when they express their love to us. So how can we approach giving and receiving love? What do we know about love? And how is it related to Dragon Energy?

### Kinds of Love

*16.1*

We can sort out seven kinds or levels of love. Going from *bottom to top* in Table 21.1 the most limited kind of love is that which is 'ordered' or demanded by an authority figure — such as in a religion or from a master to a servant — and which is not actually love.

Often called being 'in love,' the next kind is an *immature love* or *limerence* where the person is overtaken by spontaneous passion that is usually obsessive, risky, and temporary. For example, Hollywood's ideas of romantic love have twisted all of our ideas about what love is. We may have tried (before our recovery from co-dependence) to look for that 'special one' — that always seems to pop up in the movies. At first we don't know that movies are just entertainment. Becoming attached to the idea that a 'special other' may 'complete us' usually brings pain. We can find that love in our own heart for ourself. A companion ideally supports our personal and spiritual growth. But they can't fill us up. That is our job.

Once we find this supportive 'other' in our lives, we can make it romantic in a new way. We can learn what their love language is — how they give and receive love — described below. Experiencing real love is more gratifying and fulfilling, and *better than anything* from Hollywood.

The next table 16.1 summarizes more real kinds of love that we experience as friend to friend (sometimes called 'agape' love) and then parent to child love. Sibling love evolves over time, usually increasing more in adulthood if the relationship is healthy.

### Mature Love

Next in love's evolution is mature love from spouse to spouse. It develops and grows over time, involving high commitment and intimacy. Mature love is open, secure, supportive and comfortable. It is often difficult to achieve, since most couples have many of the unhealed core issues that I address throughout my book on Core Issues (some of which can manifest in adversarial ways, including 'taking each other's inventory' and other forms of argument). Unresolved, these core issues commonly trigger painful conflicts and verbal fights in relationships.

Other factors frequently trigger *Core Issues* and resulting *conflicts* as well, such as different preferences by each partner about how to best:
1) manage money and finances,
2) relate to children and other relatives,
3) decide where to live,
4) communicate with one another,
5) express sexual intimacy,

6) handle recreation and travel, and more.

When we are vulnerable, real, and can share our emotion... ...
physical pain with a safe partner who we can trust not to use
what we share with them against us, we will likely grow. Some
call this new way of being in relationship as 'being on the same
side.' Martha Beck said, 'In real life, two people who are
dwelling in Oneness never struggle. They communicate. They
share. They learn to understand one another. They're on the
same side, in a game that's played by remaining perpetually
aware that all people are One.

Table16.1 **Seven Levels of Love and Their Core Characteristics**

| Level of Love | Characteristics | Vision/Sight | Levels of Consciousness |
|---|---|---|---|
| **Highest spiritual (unconditional)** | We are love, core of our being and One with God | Visionary, creative, surrender | Unity |
| **Peaceful being** | Humility, 'Nobody special' | Clear | Compassion |
| **Spouse to spouse,** compassionate | Mature love, grows over time, high commitment and intimacy | Open, secure, supportive, comfortable | Understanding, wholeness |
| **Parent for child** | Natural, empathy | Vision of a better future | Awakening heart |
| **Friend to friend** | Spontaneous, grows | Agape love | Mutuality |
| **Immature, limerence,** "courtly love," love sickness | 'In love,' 'Smitten,' passionate, impulsive, risky obsessive, and temporary | Usually blind | Unconscious passion, 'chemistry' |
| Simple religious view, Servant to master | By commandments, Not spontaneous | To 'flock' at lower level, teaching of sin and guilt, Blind | Survival, neediness, unconscious |

When the two each heal themselves over time, work through their conflicts, gain humility and accept each other as they are, their life and their love gets easier, richer and more mature. For most of us who were never shown healthy role models for relationships, this shift from the adversarial coupleship to being on the same side and working together is at first an amazing relief and grows into a kind of love that was worth all the struggle it took to get there.

The next level of love is when we choose love over fear and we exist generally with an attitude of love for all beings and other living things. Knowing that we are 'nobody special,' we have the aid of humility. Being nobody special is confusing to our ego/intellect. We thought that becoming 'somebody special' would answer all of our wishes. But being nobody special releases us from constantly trying to keep our minds busy with how special we are. Here we feel what *A Course in Miracles* calls 'complete peace and joy.' Most of the time we feel love in our hearts and see others without judgment. We see others as struggling *spiritual beings* who are working at having a *human* experience. We are all on the same path. Some of us are further along than others, and all trying to find peace and love.

### Giving Love: Expressing Love

Gary Chapman wrote about his observations on the 'Five Love Languages,' helping people speak and understand emotional love when it is expressed directly or indirectly through any one or more of

1) words of affirmation,
2) physical touch,
3) acts of service,
4) quality time, and/or
5) receiving gifts (Table 16.2).

Chapman argues that while each of these languac
enjoyed to some degree by all people, a person will u
speak one primary love language, but all are important and
can be ranked after taking the love language profile that is
included in his book for both partners (see below).

Out of these five love languages, Chapman believed that
everyone has a primary love language. But in our
experience *many* of us have *more than one*. Check it out
for yourself.

TABLE 16.2. **The 5 Love Languages** (summarized from Chapman)

| Love Language | Examples |
|---|---|
| **Words of affirmation** | Using words to affirm the other. 'I'm so proud of you for _____!' , 'You look good in that outfit,' and the like. 'I love you' also usually works. |
| **Physical touch** | Touching, holding hands, hugging, kissing. |
| **Acts of service** | Doing things for them —from cooking, housework, fixing things – even to getting bugs off of the windshield of their car, they feel loved. |
| **Quality time** | Giving them your undivided attention. Looking into their eyes and talking is quality time. So is taking a walk or going out to eat, so long as you are communicating with each other. |
| **Receiving gifts** | The gift says, 'He/She was thinking about me. Look what they got for me.' |

To help determine what your love language(s) may be, go
online and take a survey test at
www.5lovelanguages.com/assessments /love/. Show your
results to your loved one and ask them to do the same.

From Chapman's observations, whatever makes *us* feel
loved is what *we do* or express toward our spouse. For
example, when a husband who's main love language is

physical touch comes home and goes to the kitchen, he wants his wife to feel loved. He starts hugging her. She says, 'Leave me alone! Can't you see that I am busy?' His problem is not his sincerity. He was sincere. The problem was that he was speaking *his* language and *not her* language. If acts of service is her love language, the best he might do would be to say, 'Honey, why don't you sit down and rest. Let me finish that.' Then she feels loved, since he is speaking her language.

*Another example*: A wife comes home from work to find her husband almost in tears. He tells her that his boss yelled and threatened to fire him. He is shaking. *Her* love language is words of affirmation—although neither of them understands *yet* what their love language is. She tells him what a good worker he is and how smart he is. His boss doesn't appreciate what a hard worker he is. He becomes more agitated from her words, thinking that if he's so 'good,' how come he is losing his job? At this point he's about to project his anger at his boss *onto her* because he thinks that she is making him feel worse.

If she understood that *his* love language is physical touch, she could have put her arms around him and held him until his shaking stopped. Then she might have continued to hold him while saying that if he loses his job he will find another one because he is so competent (her main love language, words of affirmation, while filling his needs to be touched). Hearing herself say that calms her down because it is true *and* what *she* also needs to hear.

*A third and final example couple* are in the same situation, but who are *both aware* of each other's love language. *His* love language is quality time. When he comes home upset and afraid, she could suggest that they go for a walk together. He may need to walk briskly until he settles down and then start to talk it out with her. She's feeling pretty threatened by his boss's words because they can't make it on her salary alone. *Her* love language is words of affirmation. So, once he calms down, he thanks her for getting him

outside and walking. *He* can also tell her that he knows they are a great team and somehow they will work this out together if he loses his job. He has gotten his quality time and she has gotten a positive sense of how the two of them are a team (on the same side, 'love and honor') and can get through this together. They are both supporting each other through this crisis instead of 'using' each other to vent their emotional pain.

These are three examples of the dynamics within this Core Issue of difficulty giving and receiving love and ways to give and receive love in a healthy way. Using these love language principles shows us how to function as a team instead of attacking one another.

## Difficulty Giving and Receiving Love

This is often the last core issue to be addressed, and for a reason. It is paradoxically both the most difficult and—ultimately after a lot of commitment and attention in a relationship—the easiest—but only after we have done the hard work through most of the other core issues.

### Reframing ~ Loving My Self ~

We can reframe the importance of loving ourself

as **self interest** and *self caring*.

Before recovery, others may have discouraged loving our self. Some of us believed we were even 'rotten to the core!' Throughout recovery we may have fought with our ego/false self often. Credible self-help books showed us how to take our life back from our false self. Sometimes it seemed that we were making headway and then we fell victim to what psychologist Bill Tollefson called 'the voice of the abuser's values' in our heads telling us all the painful material that we

were told in our childhood when we were defenseless and unable to stop all that 'junk' from coming in.

As we work through our core issues, we become more adept at dealing with these negative voices. We may realize that 'If I can't love myself, I can't love anyone else.'

→ from above Reframing

What do I need to give up to let love in?

Learning to give and receive love in healthy ways makes our life go better and raises our Dragon Energy.

*       *       *

In the next chapter Barbara continues from the cartoon of the Dragon addressing the Knights-of-old and Courtly Love on page iv.

# 17    The Power of Love – 2

We may remember Tina Turner's 1984 questioning song that asked *What's Love Got to Do with It?*'

What's love got to do, got to do with it
What's love but a sweet old fashioned notion
What's love got to do, got to do with it
Who needs a heart when a heart can be broken*

The Knights of old sitting with the Dragon in our opening cartoon and clad in their shiny armor might disagree. The legend goes that they 'loved' to be smitten by a young girl, preferably in the Queen's court and with whom they could never be physically intimate. This was called *Courtly Love*. They competed in contests of might in her name. They went to war in her name.

Legend went that the most important task they could risk for her love was to slay a Dragon. How many stories of Knights (and other masculine figures) slaying a Dragon to honor an untouchable woman have been told? How many paintings of a Damsel in Distress, locked up in a tower and include a Dragon guarding the lady so the Hero has no choice but to slay the Dragon.

From other chapters in this book, we know that these legends contain elements of truth about *us*, not Dragons. Stories of Knights and Dragons may be telling us something about us.

On page 42 we said, 'Once we slay our Dragon as our *attachment to our own ego*, then we become progressively *less inhibited*, more spontaneous and free to be Real and identify with the Eastern Dragon to enliven our natural Creative Energy.'

Through these Courtly Love myths we learn again that the Dragon is our attachment to our own ego. To love, to love deeply love with no impediments – the kind of love that God wishes for us, we need to address our old 'baggage' that we may be carrying without our awareness until now when we want to and are ready to Love with a capital L.

Here's how regular 'love' has been for most of us. We love the way someone new looks, smells, laughs at our jokes, etc. We 'fall in love.' We are smitten. We date. We know this is it! We have sex. This intensity is usually temporary, called Limerence. *Limerence* is a state of mind which results from a romantic attraction to another person and typically includes obsessive thoughts and fantasies and a desire to form or maintain a relationship with the object of love and have one's feelings reciprocated.

But our old wounding or baggage is now in bed with us and continues to follow us around until we both work through our own 'stuff' (rare), or we break up because everything they are 'Mirroring' back to us is obviously their fault!

'Healthy' friendships that evolve into a romantic physical relationship go from 'healthy' to ego centered. This is because we are activating our lower chakras where most of our unfinished business (ego) is stored.

## Letting Go of ego

Whenever we have let go of our Dragon ego we are ready for what I am describing here. Whenever we share a relationship that changes us for the better we might call it *'Dragon Love.'* We like who we are now and this other person mirrors that back to us. The texture is different. And it's bigger than us. It may never be sexual or it may. Both of us are comfortable with the way it is.

Without sex, we can celebrate Agape [A-ga-pei], *love as a pledge.*

These relationships imprint on us. We create new circuits in our brain. We also create or activate the connection between our heart and our mind. Sometimes, it awakens the heart's mind (as in, 'My heart told me so').

We are touched in a way that we know we will never be the same. When we 'slay our own Dragon', when each of us lets go of our own ego, we can each grow and watch our partner doing the same.

Ken Ring interviewed me in 1982 for his breakthrough book *Heading Toward Omega* and a few years later for *Lessons from the Light.* Shortly thereafter, I moved to Connecticut for six years for the Near-Death Studies Research with Bruce Greyson, MD at the University of Connecticut Medical School. For that time, Ken and I lived in the same area.

Ken and I have thanked each other many times since for all the good we gave each other. In this email below, he called me 'Dragon Lady' and then as I re-read what we were telling each other, I knew this chapter for this book was coming. It's about the special Energy that's fitting in to our mythological idea of courtly love, slaying the Dragon and Dragon Energy.

I write about meeting Ken Ring and his NDE research on page 140 above. Next he is referring to that story.

Ken: I had a chance to read that excerpt from your chapter just now, Barbara. Yes, it certainly brought back memories. I think with all those visits to you (when I still lived in Florida) and the special connection we were developing then, some readers may well think that we were actually having an affair at the time! And in a way, I guess we were — a spiritual love affair and a deep connection between us.          Love, Ken

Barbara answers: I have been asked by old friends if we had an affair and I said 'Yes' — but a deeper affair than what they may think.

Ours has always been an affair of the heart. Sex would have gotten in the way, bringing up all those old issues that plague us until we work them through. Our relationship has always felt like deep soul understanding and connection.

So glad we can both acknowledge our special love.
Love, Barbara

In looking back at several of my relationships, without Dragon Energy we were numb to all the benefits of slaying our ego (small d) dragon.

With Dragon Energy, we let-our-ego-go, face our issues by naming and owning them, not projecting them on to the other person. We realize together that we are helping each other grow because we are now rooted in Unconditional Love—we love the other person just the way they are and we identify any core issues that might be troubling to us as **ours** to work through.

While writing this chapter I had lunch with our oldest grandchild, Jacob who was here visiting from his home in Florida. He was telling me about Michelle his wife. (She is one of the sweetest kindest women I know. I always love her company.) He was telling me about her love of Dragons, including all kinds of figurines, etc. Then a few minutes later he described Michelle as one of the most fun loving people he knows. He said, 'She makes every day an adventure. The most ordinary things become extraordinary.'

This was another example of love as a real Power of Dragon Energy.

## Michelangelo Phenomenon  *

The Michelangelo phenomenon or effect is an experience some psychologists found and reported in which interdependent people influence and 'sculpt' each other.

Over time, the Michelangelo effect causes individuals to develop toward what they themselves consider as their 'ideal selves'. For example, in a close relationship, 'because John affirms Mary's ideals, Mary increasingly comes to resemble her ideal self'.

---

* The phenomenon was named after the Italian Renaissance painter, sculptor, architect, poet and engineer Michelangelo (1475–1564) who is said to have thought of sculpting as a process of revealing and uncovering the figures hidden in stone. The term was introduced in 1999 by the US psychologist Stephen Michael Drigotas.

The Michelangelo phenomenon is related to the looking-glass self-concept introduced by Charles Horton Cooley in his 1902 work *Human Nature and the Social Order* and is referred to in contemporary marital therapy. Recent popular work in couples therapy and conflict resolution points to the importance of the Michelangelo phenomenon. Diana Kirschner reported that the phenomenon was common among couples reporting high levels of marital satisfaction.

# 18  *Victim to Survivor to Thriver* and *Dragon Energy*

I (BW) wrote my 6th book *Victim to Survivor and Thriver* in 2011 (summarized in Table 18.5 2 pages below). At the time, I was unaware that to become a Survivor I could call my healing work also as using my earliest Dragon Energy. To become and be a Thriver — I needed to move under and beyond all 3 of the Veils that we show on page 7 illustrated so well by Ciruelo. All of the characteristics in the Thriver column below describe features of 4 D and 5 D living as we show on page 184.

Years later we found a good graphic illustration of the V → S →T process of healing that we show on the next page. Of course the first figure represents the Victim, then the Survivor and then Thriver. We note that the Thriver is looking upward and with humility as though to a Higher Power.

This process goes back to and is similar to that of • ancient and current Alchemy, • working through the Chakras and • spans to our current 2019 trauma recovery of *Adult Children of Alcoholics* [*and trauma*] and which we have published on since 1987 as *Healing the Child Within, A Gift to Myself* and several other books.

Figure 18. **The V → S → T Process**

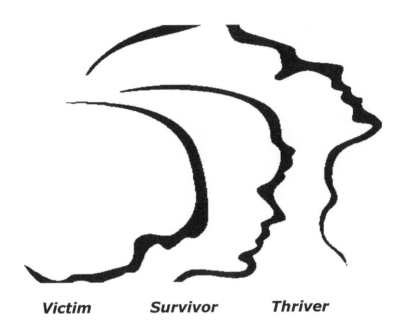

*Victim*          *Survivor*          *Thriver*

Table 18.1 **Direction of Dragon Energy in Healing and Evolution**

| Victim | Survivor | Thriver |
|---|---|---|
| 'Depression' | Movement of feelings | Dragon Energy |
| Doesn't deserve to enjoy life | Struggling to heal | Gratitude for everything in life |
| Low self-esteem/ shame/ unworthy | Sees self as wounded *and* healing | Sees self as overflowing miracle |
| Hyper-vigilant | Learning to relax | Experiences peace |
| Confusion and numbness | Learning to grieve, grieving past ungrieved traumas | Grieving current hurts, losses and traumas |
| Hopeless | Hopeful | Trusts Real Self and life |
| Hides personal story | Tells their story to safe people | Transforms story to Hero's Journey |
| Feels Defective | Compassion for others and eventually self | Open heart for self and others |
| Often hurt by unsafe others | Learning how to protect self by "share-check-share" | Protects self from unsafe others |
| Own needs come last | Learning healthy needs | Makes self first |
| Allows repeated dramas | Sees drama patterns | Creates peace |
| Believes suffering is the human condition | Feels some relief | Finds peace and joy |
| Always serious, can't laugh | Beginning to laugh | *Experiences* healthy humor |
| Inappropriate humor, teasing | Feels appropriate painful feelings | *Uses* healthy humor |
| Numb or angry around toxic people | Increased awareness of pain and dynamics | Healthy boundaries with all people |
| Lives in the past | Aware of patterns | Lives in the Now |
| Angry at religion | Understanding the difference between religion & spirituality | Dragon Energy = Natural Spirituality |

From Whitfield B 2011 *Victim to Survivor and Thriver* Muse House Press, Atlanta GA

# EPILOGUE

We end with this short story below. It has a huge theme that not only underlies this book, but also underlies all of our books, papers and private practice helping victims of trauma evolve into survivors and finally thrivers.

## Eternal Circle of the Soul

### Barbara Harris Whitfield

Once upon a time, a long time ago, before you and I were born, I was a little spark of light, a twinkle in God's eye. I got the news one day that I was to report again down here for another stint.

'Wait a minute. Wait a minute!' Of course 'wait a minute' was just a figure of speech because there is no time when you are a twinkle in God's eye. There is no time in eternity.

'Wait a minute,' I said, 'I don't want to do that again. I always wind up getting knocked around. This human business is no piece of cake, you know!' God smiled and a tear formed in God's eye, which washed me out. I rolled down God's cheek and God caught the tear in God's hand and held it up to see me.

'You're right,' God said. 'It's not too good where the humans are. But we want them to remember that they are like you and me. They need to remember that they are Light and God, too. You need to go down there and help them remember.'

'All right,' I said, wincing. 'But am I going to have to forget again who I am like I always do? Can I skip that part, please?' 'No,' God said, 'but I can offer you something a little different this time. You can have a peaceful life, even a happy life, as soon as you remember. It might take a while, but always choose the highest good and I'll lead. They need to remember that they are Light and God, too. You need to go down there and help them remember.'

ıl right,' I said, wincing, 'But am I going to have to forget again who I am like I always do? Can I skip that part, please?' 'No, 'God said, 'but I can offer you something a little different this time. You can have a peaceful life, even a happy life, as soon as you remember. It might take a while, but always choose the highest good and I'll lead you to peaceful, happy times.

'How will I know the highest good?' I pleaded.

'Just say to yourself, "What would God do?" And I promise you I will answer. Just listen very carefully to the softest voice within.'

'What a deal,' I whined. 'I don't want to go back. I get so lonely.'
God got another tear in God's eye because I talked about being lonely.

God wiped the tear with God's other hand and we both saw another twinkle. It was you saying, 'I don't want to leave God. Put me back!'

God looked at you and said, 'You need to be a human again.'

'Oh no,' you said. 'Not again. Do I have to forget who I am and all about you again? And, I get so lonely. It's not easy being human, you know. None of the others really understand yet what being human means!'

God smiled and then said to you, 'Always pick the highest good and you will find yourself fast. And when you remember me, ask for this...' And God took both hands and put them together so both tears became one. We were the brightest twinkle God had ever seen.'

God laughed a big laugh and said, 'All right, my bright twinkles. You are going off separately now to try being human again, and when you remember to always pick the highest good, I will help you to remember your Soul and Me. And I promise you that if you do that, it will make two tears in my eyes come together and then you will find each other and be the brightest beam of Light. Oh! This is going to be Good!'

And God smiled again.'
It seems like that was eons ago. But here we are, two together again. God kept God's promise. It took us a little while to figure it all out, but

occasionally when you look in my eyes, there are two tears that become one because I look back into yours and I can feel God's smile in my heart.

*      *      *

This little story illustrates the Soulful thoughts we are ending with:
1) If we always choose the highest good,
2) and learn to listen to the softest voice within, then,
3) we live as our natural Soul
4) and the more Soul family we will meet."
5) Living this way, in communion with a God Source introduces us to peace and contentment and when things are going well -- Joy.

The main point is to always choose the highest good which can be understood if we ask ourselves, 'What would God do?' Or 'What does God want me to do?' And then wait for the gentle voice within to answer.

### A Wish for You

Life is a miracle
And beautiful, too.
We wish you who are reading now
This experience over and over again.
We hope you find your Soul and Its family.
We wish you peace in your hearts
And the vision that comes from seeing
Through God's eyes,
The eyes of our
Sacred
Eternal
Natural Soul.

Excerpt From: Barbara Harris Whitfield. *The Natural Soul.*

# GLOSSARY

*[handwritten annotations: strong and dramatic / Art, Age regression Suddenly feel upset, confused & scared like a helpless little child.]*

**Abreaction** – An opportunity to heal. Common and important. *Reliving a trauma* experience from our unconscious mind to purge it of its emotional excesses. An attempt to heal from the trauma effects if the person or clinician names and analyzes it in the person's life. Often it is a method of becoming conscious of repressed traumatic events. Commonly triggered by a related experience and mis-diagnosed as a 'mental illness.' Drains Dragon Energy unless name and work through it, when DE increases.

**Absorption** – Complete interest in something. First, we dissociate from this current reality, become absorbed in the different reality and seem to move into it. A key element in the Flow state (page 119).

***A Course in Miracles*** – *see Miracle*

**Archetype** – A universal symbolic pattern and more. Archetypal characters and stories appear repeatedly in myths across many diverse cultures. These folk legends are exposing our collective inner life. Developed by Carl Jung and James Hillman, archetypal psychology recognizes the myriad myths and fantasies that shape and are shaped by our psychological lives (page 83).

**Alchemy –** An ancient term for psycho-spiritual transformation, healing and growth, sometimes used today for that meaning. It embodied the '*chemistry' of inner union. Learning* about Dragon Energy and *activating* it is an alchemical process. Commonly *mistaken* as an early and mis-understood, unscientific form of chemistry that *on the surface* sought to change base metals into gold and discover a life-prolonging elixir, a universal cure for disease and a universal solvent (that some called 'alkahest') able to dissolve every other substance, including gold. The 17th c. scientist Isaac Newton liked to look everywhere for how things worked. He often *looked under* conventional scientific assumptions, which led to many of his great discoveries. This 'looking-under' to find truths was a key to his using Alchemy (the *chemistry of inner union* that used the scientific skill of 'looking under' early assumptions). At the time Europe was dominated by the Church's power – why Alchemists as Newton used it to survive politically. Alchemy started along with the Gnostics – an early Christian group, both early in 1st 2 centuries AD/CE looking for spirituality outside the Churches' dictates.

**Ayurveda** - Practiced in India for millennia by the Hindu; means life-knowledge. It reveals the path to ultimate well-being by identifying our individual characteristics and patterns of health, showing how to bring balance in our life. Uses Yoga, meditation, positive thinking and more.

An ancient practical and spiritual science that we also relate to Dragon Energy.

**Being Real** - A healthy self-expression that helps us in *Naming* all these things and experiences. Counteracts the stress of living in co-dependence. When we name them (people, places and things) Right, Correctly or Accurately, this is a key to living in 4 D living and then thriving in 5 D. *our newly awakened (pages 19-20), XVFF*

**Boundary** – Where you end and I begin. A limit of practical everyday use with people, places and things that helps our life go better. If another 'invades' our boundaries, it can feel uncomfortable to maddening.

**Caduceus** – The symbol of medicine, nursing, and related healing professions that employs the snake/Dragon overlying the vertical staff with wings atop, all of which also represent Kundalini energy, which we describe in some detail (page 93ff).

**Chakras** – Consciousness and growth points found within the subtle body (see below and page 93ff). These growth points parallel • Maslow's hierarchy of needs, and they parallel • our levels of consciousness and • the Stages of Recovery (page 160 ) and interweave with • the Twelve Steps. *12 ff*

**Co-dependence** – Focusing on others to our detriment. The most common relationship problem. The Core Issue of *Difficulty Being Real* is at its base. *which include most of*

**Common Sense** – Dragon Energy runs on common sense. See characteristics (p. 23-24)

**Consciousness** – Is aware *existence or being*, which is fundamentally conscious. Awareness of being aware. The part of us that watches the watcher. Meditation and prayer increase our awareness of it. A *Divine Mystery* that over time searches to know itself, others and God better.

**'Contempt prior to investigation'** – Some AA (Alcoholics Anonymous) members have quoted this saying to reflect their own past denial and how they may see some of the people they sponsor ('sponsee,' 'pigeon'). The 4-word phrase can apply to anyone who intensely denies anything that could involve them or others. 'There is a principle which is a bar against all information, which is proof against all arguments and which cannot fail to keep a man in everlasting ignorance —

that principle is *contempt prior to investigation.*' - Herbert Spencer / William Paley from the 1800s

**Creative** – Making new ideas or things, often from old ones.

*(pages 109 & 117)*

**Creativity** – The *process* of making new ideas or things from old ones. A basic characteristic and power in Dragon Energy.

**Dimensions** – Usually means measurements of length, height, width and depth, which defines part of what some call 3 D existence. Other observers and we expand 3D into 4D and 5D, which are the highest realization of Dragon Energy (page 19-20). See also ***Intent*** below.

*Smaller font if need*

**Dissociation** - Separation from our feelings and emotions, whether joyous or painful. A process whereby our *experience* of something — incoming, stored or outgoing—is actively *deflected from* our *focused awareness* and our *assimilation* or *integration* with its ordinary, usual or expected mental associations. Happens commonly across a spectrum of healthy to unhealthy.  *experiences, memory,*

**Dragon** - A mythical creature that represents traits that are also within and parts of us. The most written about, talked about, drawn, painted, sculpted and represented creature in public and private media of all time. The most celebrated phantasy creature of all time, all coming from our mind's creative imagination. Could all this have come about from our inherent Dragon Energy?

*own        + collective*

**Dragon Energy** - What we each have and can recognize, activate and strengthen within our consciousness at any time. We describe it in detail throughout this book. *See page 23ff.*

**Dragon Energy Love** - An expanded view of love. How we love ourselves, others and God when we are healthy, balanced and see the world with Humility. We lack nothing — without our needing someone or something to fill in our empty places. Living in DE, the world and our life is experienced in 5D. We naturally have gratitude and when it spills over it turns into Joy.

**Divine Mystery** — Each of us. You, I, all. In relationship to God.

**Energy** - Quantum physics has shown us that a microcosm exists that is mostly space with microscopic particles (that can also be waves) that are constantly moving and forming the illusion of material things. The movements are what we call 'energy.' Everything in the Universe is made of this energy, *each of us ,*

*as are*

**Esoteric** — Hidden to others. The 'inner' (eso-), in the sense of inner consciousness; the contemplative, mystical or meditative transpersonal perspective. Experienced only by intuition or high mental or spiritual faculties. Teacher Tom Hickey said 'All true Esotericism is *Gnostic*. That is, it is based on Higher Knowledge, or *Gnosis*, to use the Greek term. Gnosis is viewed by some as a better way of understanding than Reason.

**Exoteric** — Not hidden. Knowledge that is outside and independent from a person's experience and can be ascertained by anyone and related to common sense.

**Freedom** — A necessary personal and public space to experience Dragon Energy. Having the ability to act or change without constraint.

God/Goddess/All that Is

**God** – Unlimited intelligent Energy, totally non-judgmental, pure Love. Many names for. When we connect with experientially, increases all our Energy, including Dragon Energy.

**Gratitude** – A spiritual skill to reframe our life experiences in a positive direction. Expressing it in prayer usually pays off and raises our Dragon Energy.

**Guru** – An ancient and current Sanskrit term for teacher, counselor, spiritual guide, expert or master of knowledge within a field. Traditionally a reverential figure to the student who helps mold values, shares experiential knowledge as much as literal knowledge, an exemplar in life, an inspirational source. The goal is to find our own inner guru, which is usually our Real Self experientially connected to God. (Beware of false teachers, professors, priests, or politicians who exploit their students' vulnerabilities. These false gurus have sociopathic traits and negative Dragon Energy. To avoid being exploited by them — find your Real Self and maintain healthy boundaries around all teachers.)

**Heart** – Term used to describe the emotional aspects of our Real Self.

**Hermeneutics** — Academic term for *Interpretation*. The theory and methodology of interpretation, especially in the interpretation of biblical texts, wisdom literature, and philosophical texts. Modern hermeneutics includes both verbal and non-verbal communication as well as semiotics, presuppositions, and pre-understandings. Hermeneutics has been broadly applied in the humanities, especially in law, history and theology.

**Human** – From back around 5,000 years ago we humans began to make the Dragon via our creative imagination — unknowingly based on that it represents traits that are also within us. This important connection is in part why we wrote this book, from which we hope you will profit and enjoy. See pages 33, 93 84,

**Humility** – The openness to learn more about our self, others and God. A skill and power that inherently resides in our mind and increases our Dragon Energy. When we let go of our ego.

**Hundredth Monkey effect** – Idea that a momentum develops when enough of us hold something to be true, it becomes true for everyone. (Based on research with monkeys on a northern Japanese Island, that when enough individuals in a population adopt a new idea or behavior, there occurs an ideological breakthrough that allows this new awareness to be communicated directly from mind to mind without the connection of external experience and then *all* individuals in the population spontaneously adopt it. Political correctness is one among many examples of the Hundredth Monkey effect.)

**Imaginal** – Does not mean imaginary. Healthy Dissociation is the doorway to the Imaginal realm. It is a realm where in our creative imagination the fairies, leprechauns and Dragons exist. Over the course of human evolution many sane, successful and creative people have dipped into this realm or dimension to create a kind of consensual validation. Crossing over into this realm helps to prime the pump of our *creativity*.

**Imaginal Realm** – Where dreams, myth and synchronicity help us realign soulfully to the natural world and to our innate wholeness. The area within and around the 3 Veils and the subsequent 5 D alpha Dragon Energy on the other side. Ken Ring wrote '...with the imaginal realm, we are *not* talking of the stuff of fantasy or even "imagination," as these terms are generally used today. Specifically, we are not concerned here with fictive matters or what is "made up" through creative invention. Instead, the imaginal realm refers to a *third kingdom,* access to which is dependent neither on sensory perception nor on normal waking cognition (including fantasy). Because it lies hidden from common view, it can usually be apprehended only in what we now call certain *altered states of consciousness* that have the effect of undermining ordinary perception and conceptual thinking. When these are sufficiently disturbed, the imaginal realm, like the starry night sky that can be discerned only when sunset is absent, stands revealed." Ring p 220 See also *Liminal* below. Heading Toward One a

**Individuation** – The main task of human development which we describe from several perspectives as the evolution of psycho-spiritual growth and a basic goal of each of us as we find and live our healthy Dragon Energy. The process wherein our mind/consciousness/self develops from birth out of an early undifferentiated self – during which our immature ego (negative ego) helps us survive while our mind explores our experiences. If the process is more or less successful and integrated over time into a well-functioning whole, the healing is a success. [Same as Alchemy, which Jung understood and supported.] ... From Jung through Maslow and to our work.

**Intention**, Intentional – *Thought* effects the reality of all sorts from almost all our mental, physical, relationships, meaning and life outcomes. Synonyms: Intent, aim, purpose, goal, target, objective, plan. How we move out of 3 D then through **4 D** and into **5 D**. (See also page 19). A sizable body of research exploring the nature of consciousness for more than thirty years in scientific institutions around the world shows that thoughts are capable of affecting everything from the simplest machines to the most complex living beings. This evidence suggests that human thoughts and intentions are an actual physical 'something' with the astonishing power to change our world. Every thought we have is a tangible *energy* with the *power* to transform. A thought is not only a thing; it is a thing that *influences other things*.
This central idea, that consciousness affects matter, lies at the very heart of an irreconcilable difference between the worldview offered by classical physics—the science of the big, visible world—and that of quantum physics: the science of the world's most diminutive components. That difference concerns the very nature of matter and the ways it can be influenced to change." from Science journalist Lynne McTaggart *The Intention Experiment* We must also recognize that these ideas are no longer the ruminations of a few eccentric individuals. The power of *thought* underpins many well-accepted disciplines in every reach of life, from orthodox and alternative medicine to competitive sport. Modern medicine must fully appreciate the central role of intention in healing. Medical scientists often speak of the "placebo effect" as an annoying impediment to the proof of the efficacy of a chemical agent. It is time that we understood and made full use of the power of the placebo. Repeatedly, the mind has proved to be a far more powerful healer than the greatest of breakthrough drugs. See **Thoughts** below.


**Jung**, Carl (1875-1961) – A pioneering and influential Swiss MD psychiatrist and psychoanalyst who was influential in psychiatry, anthropology, archaeology, literature, philosophy, and religious studies. The cure as we understand Jung is to *discover meaning in one's life through experience* – follow your convictions and *learn* by what happens next. Above all, choose love, faith, hope and insight instead of sexuality, fear, disillusionment and pseudo-consciousness. 'A plain-spoken sage he could be at times, deep, elegant and never denying our capacity for both good and evil.'

Among the central concepts of analytical psychology is *individuation* - the lifelong psychological process of differentiation of the self out of each individual's conscious and unconscious elements. Jung considered individuation to be the main task of human development. He created well known psychological concepts, including synchronicity, archetypal phenomena, the collective unconscious, the psychological complex, and extraversion and introversion.

**Kinesiology** — is based on the theory is that all living things have an energy field. This energy field is connected to all other energy fields in some way or another. In short, we are all connected to each other in some way. Nothing we say or do or that has been said, done or felt occurs in a vacuum and so has an effect on energy. Because of this, everything that is or was is written into an energy record of the collective unconscious. The problem is how to access this information.

*small font*

**Kundalini** – A cultural and spiritual name from the ancient Sanskrit language for the generic Energy talked about in most world religions. It is the natural energy within us that helps us to grow, evolve and become all of who we are meant to be. Eastern medical models incorporate this energy into their healing modalities, i.e., in acupuncture, yoga and some forms of energy massage. Many people who work with the energy compare it to the Christian *Holy Spirit*, the Native American *Great Spirit* or the Hebrew term *Ruach ha Kadosh*. These are all terms we have given to the *same unconditionally loving Energy* of God. We believe that this Energy is also a key part of *Dragon Energy*. It is the healthy connection to self, others and the God-of-our-understanding, a bridge that eventually leads us to experience Oneness. We can sometimes physically feel it, especially when we are in a creative act. Although the modern Caduceus symbol of medicine exemplifies Kundalini, most health professionals don't know what it means.

**Liminal** - In anthropology, *liminality* (from the Latin *līmen*, meaning 'a *threshold*') is the quality of *ambiguity* or *disorientation* that occurs in the middle stage of a rite of passage, when participants no longer hold their pre-ritual status but have not yet begun the *transition* to the status they will hold when the rite is complete. During a rite's liminal stage, participants 'stand at the *threshold*' between their previous way of structuring their identity, time or community, and a new way, which completing the rite establishes. Belonging to the point of conscious awareness below or above, which something cannot be experienced or felt. See Imaginal.

(P171).

**Love** – An overused concept that usually has strings attached. There are levels of love. ~~Pure love has no strings.~~ The lovers are without needs or demands and see and accept each other unconditionally.

**Courtly Love** — We love others for who they are without needing or wanting anything back from them. We honor and serve another selflessly. See page 177.

169 ave

**Meditation** – Observer-self training. Helps clear ego and mind and lessen worry. Aloneness in silence. Increases focus, decision making and creativity. Increases Dragon Energy.

**Metaphysical** — Beyond the physical. Topics of metaphysical investigation include existence, objects and their properties, space and time, cause and effect and possibility. A realm that Dragon Energy seekers visit.

**Mind** (Human) - ***Where everything happens***. It is the activating agent of our Spirit, creativity, negativity (ego attachment, wrong mind), positivity (Right Mind [from *A Course in Miracles*]). P xxix

**Mindfulness** - Paying *attention* in a particular way; on purpose, in the *present moment*, and *nonjudgment*ally. From Jon Kabat-Zinn

**Mystical** *experience* – from William James criteria – see page 201.

**Miracle** from *A Course in Miracles* – The Course defines a miracle as – the peace we experience when we choose God over our ego. Our peace then reverberates to our close others – supporting personal harmony. (In *The Course* a miracle is *Not*, e.g., feeding the multitudes with one fish or making wine from water.)

**Nadi**s – Sanskrit term for psycho-spiritual circulatory channels within the body – *similar* to veins, arteries, the respiratory system, the nervous system, the digestive system, the excretory system, and the reproductive system. Think of *nadis* as the information highway to your mind, body, soul, and spirit, just as the Internet is the information highway that brings information to your browser. The Net cannot help you grow psycho-spiritually, while Kundalini through the Nadis does.

**Naming things correctly** – A powerful practice from and as our Real Self that increases our Dragon Energy and gives us more peace over time. Opposite of PC. When we name them (people, places and things) Right, Correctly or Accurately, this is a key to 4 D living and then thriving in 5 D.

**One Day at a Time** – One of the most profound principles of healing is embodied in this simple phrase. Although healing takes a long time, by using this reminder, our outlook can shift immediately, making the journey not only more tolerable, but meaningful, and anchoring us in the present moment. As we grieve our buried pain and work through our core recovery issues, with patience we will slowly release our past unresolved internal conflicts. We gradually discover that our future is a destination not yet determined. Our life is in the present, which is where we can eventually find peace. *(see pages 123 & 4).*

**People, Places & Things** – Simplest list of addictions and unhealthy attachments as described throughout the Twelve Step process and experience.

**Political correctness** – A form of *self*-censorship and *group*-censorship that minimizes, misrepresents, distorts and/or falsifies what we observe and experience. A curtailment of freedom of speech that places *limits on debates* in the public arena (*Encyclopedia Britannica*). PC is a form of censorship that starts and maintains the un-freedom of political coercive systems of socialism, communism and Nazi-ism (Michael William 2016 *The Genesis of Political Correctness*: The Basis of a False Morality). Living in the *PC trap* drains all our energy and it lowers our Dragon Energy. This is in part because Being Real is a primary and key characteristic of Dragon Energy.

**Portal** — A doorway, gateway or entry to something else. See section on 4 Dimensional living and being, here to 5 D (pages 19 & 20).

**Power** — Term describing important areas within which to identify and raise our Dragon Energy. Throughout this book we describe and elaborate on how to use our **mind's** many ***powers***. These powers include several parts of our inner life and *how to handle* our ***relationships*** — whether good or bad — with *people*, *places* and *things* in our outer life.

**Psyche** — Ancient Greek term for the totality of the human mind, conscious and unconscious. Derived meanings included spirit, soul and real self.

**Re-Enactment** (*Repetition Compulsion*) – Repeating the same action, usually mistakes, over and over.

**Reframe** – A skill of our mind to 'make lemonade out of lemons.' Healthy reframing increases Dragon Energy. *Examples*: • Reframe 'anxiety' as fear and address what I am afraid of. • Reframe 'depression' as how I am feeling and functioning and talk to a safe person as a therapist or counselor. Reframing is a way of viewing and experiencing events, ideas, concepts and emotions to find more positive alternatives. See also http://changingminds.org/techniques/general/reframing.htm

**Reverie** — Lost-in-thought, thinking pleasant thoughts, daydreaming, wondering, contemplating, musing, imagining, being miles away, fantasizing. All often are part of creative process.

*↑ out*

**Safe person or relationship** – Someone who listens and does not give you advice, shame you or try to change you. *(see page 166)*

**Samadhi** - The unity of the subject and the object, the inner and the outer world, our Self and the Absolute. The gradual unity of consciousness and existence. Another term for enlightenment. *Be wary of anyone claiming to be fully attained,*

*social and*

**Science** – Generic term for whatever a specialty field wants to use to embellish or strengthen itself. These include a spectrum from the natural or 'hard' sciences (e.g., biology, chemistry, and physics), which study nature in the broadest sense; the social 'sciences' (e.g., economics, psychology, and sociology), which study individuals and societies; and the formal sciences (e.g., logic, mathematics, and theoretical computer science), which study abstract concepts. There is disagreement on whether the formal sciences actually constitute a science as they do not rely on *empirical* evidence (*observation* via *senses*). Disciplines that use existing scientific knowledge for practical purposes, such as engineering and medicine, are described as applied sciences. See chapter 1 on how to use science to access and prove your Dragon Energy.

**Shadow** – Where we store all of our unfinished business. From Jung - *self-knowledge as a psycho therapeutic measure frequently requires* much painstaking work extending over a long period. (From *Aion: Phenomenology of the Self*-published in *The Portable Jung,* edited by Joseph Campbell, Penguin Books, 1976, p. 145.)

**Social media** — An internet-based pre-programmed — by owners and not by us — algorithm hiding behind the word 'media' when much is about their opinions and censorship of our free speech. A double-edged sword. Most owners spy or snoop on mostly unknowing users to get our posted information to get our money and censor our words.

**Soul** - A term, similar to Spirit, with multiple meanings and dimensions for our Real Self especially when we live eternally.

**Spiritual** – Referring to the transcendent, nonphysical, divine, sacred human experiences. Right brain associations make it easier to recognize. Always there when we open to it from our heart or spirit.

**Spirituality** – Experience and practice of the spiritual. Strengthens and expands and our Dragon Energy.

**Spirit** – A term with multiple meanings and dimensions for our life-force. A part of and activated by our mind.

**Story** — Classically in our story is in 3 parts: What we were like, What happened and What we're like now.

**Subtle body** — An energetic, psycho-spiritual system within the body of several layers of increasing subtlety and metaphysical significance through which we seek knowledge of our self and the nature of God. Not a material body, but commonly occurs within and affects our body. Not visible to our eyes, but it is visible to our consciousness by our life experience. Ancient traditions of both the East and West have long maintained that the human being is a complex of material and nonmaterial systems, or energy bodies. In many of these traditions, the component parts of the subtle body serve as a map of the different levels of consciousness. (Used in such healing methods as Acupuncture, Alternative medicine, Spiritual counseling, Alchemy, Ayurveda, Tantra, Qi Gong, Chakra work and Yoga. In medicine it is reflected in the medical Caduceus [pages 93ff])

**Synchronicity** –A meaningful coincidence that if looked at — and through Dragon Energy — can have positive messages for us. Sometimes called 'surprises' that can spark creativity. (For advanced seekers, see Conjunctions of Meaningfully Parallel Events [CMPEs]).

**'The Force'** – Another term with multiple meanings and dimensions for our life-force. Popularized by George Lucas in *Star Wars* books and movies in various ways. Religious studies professor Jennifer Porter called The Force a metaphor for godhood that resonates and inspires within [people] a deeper commitment to the godhood identified within their traditional faith.

**The Tao** – The Way, pronounced 'Dao' means literally the path or way. It is a *universal principle* that underlies everything from the creation of galaxies to the interaction of human beings. The workings of Tao are vast and often beyond human logic. In order to understand Tao, reasoning alone will not suffice. One must step outside the box and apply a kind of 6th sense bordering on intuition. In our study of Tao, our source material is *Tao Te Ching* (pronounced "Dao De Jing") by the ancient sage Laozi, a.k.a. Lao Tzu. Get a copy and find out how to navigate it.

**Thoughts** – Among the most powerful actions of our Mind. Are early in the **common string** of how most parts of our **inner life** **unfold** after first starting as our ● *beliefs*, which lead to → our ● *thoughts*, which generate → our ● *feelings*, which influence → our ● *decisions*, which lead to → our ● *choices*, then to → our ● *behaviors*, each of which are all parts of our inner and finally our outer **life experiences** (Lazaris). See also *Political Correctness* above to address the *PC thought police*.

**Trauma** - occurs when any act, event or experience harms or damages any one or more of our *physical*, sexual, *mental*, emotional or *spiritual* integrity that resides within the sanctity of our True Self. No one lives a full life without having experienced hurts, losses and traumas. Those of us who recognize and *name* them and then heal from their sometimes disabling effects end up with the strongest Dragon Energy. Safe relationships support healing.

**Truth** — Generic term for what we each or as a group want to be true — for whatever concern we or they choose. Our personal truth is inside us as our Real Self, True Identity, and consciousness. Our Mind can help us find our truths (page 29ff).

**Twelve Step process** — A powerful and never-ending series of remembering, contemplating, working, sharing and reflecting on these powerful 214 words of the Steps. Related to levels of consciousness, the Chakra system and Spirituality.

**Unconscious Mind** — A collection of unknown or forgotten experiences and especially trauma after effects.

**Veil** — a transition point in psycho-spiritual *describe* growth as we in the *Special Section* (page 7). 5 - 9

**Vulnerability-** The part of us that puts our fear behind when we need courage. We act without fear so that our Dragon Energy can act unrestricted. See page 144 about Ciruelo's painting called 'Flight Instructors.'

# APPENDIX

## 1      Our Only Enemy is ...

### Our false self or ego

This false or co-dependent self or ego appears to be universal among humans. It has been described or referred to countless times in print and in our daily lives. It has been called such diverse names as a survival tool, psychopathology, the egocentric ego and the impaired or defensive self. It can be destructive to self, others and intimate relationships. It is a double-edged sword. It has some uses. But just how useful is it? And under what circumstances?

The following poem by Charles C. Finn describes many of our struggles with our false self.

### Please Hear What I'm Not Saying

Don 't be fooled by me.
Don't be fooled by the face I wear.
For I wear a mask, a thousand masks, masks that I'm afraid to take off,
and none of them is me.
Pretending is an art that's second nature with me. But don't be fooled.
For God's sake don't be fooled.
I give you the impression that I'm secure,
that all is sunny and unruffled with me, within as well as without,
that confidence is my name and coolness my game, that the water's calm and
I'm in command, and that I need no one.
But don't believe me.
My surface may seem smooth but my surface is my mask,
ever-varying and ever-concealing.
Beneath lays no complacence.
Beneath lays confusion and fear and aloneness.
But I hide this. I don't want anybody to know it.
I panic at the thought of my weakness and fear being exposed.
That's why I frantically create a mask to hide behind, a nonchalant sophisticated
facade, to help me pretend, to shield me from the glance that knows.
But such a glance is precisely my salvation. My only hope and I know it.
That is, if it's followed by acceptance, if it's followed by love.

It's the only thing that can liberate me from myself, from my own self-built
prison walls, from the barriers I so painstakingly erect.
It's the only thing that will assure me of what I can't assure myself,
that I'm really worth something.
But I don't tell you this. I don't dare. I'm afraid to.
I'm afraid your glance will not be followed by acceptance,
will not be followed by love.
I 'm afraid you'll think less of me, that you'll laugh, and your laugh would kill me.
I'm afraid that deep-down I'm nothing, that I'm just no good,
and that you will see this and reject me.
So I play my game, my desperate pretending game,
with a facade of assurance without and a trembling child within.
So begins the glittering but empty parade of masks,
and my life becomes a front.
I idly chatter to you in the suave tones of surface talk.
I tell you everything that's really nothing, and nothing of what's everything,
of what's crying within me.
So when I'm going through my routine, do not be fooled by what I'm saying.
Please listen carefully and try to hear what I'm not saying,
what I'd like to be able to say, what for survival I need to say,
but what I can't say.
I don't like to hide. I don't like to play superficial phony games.
I want to stop playing them.
I want to be genuine and spontaneous and me, but you've got to help me.
You've got to hold out your hand even when that's the last thing I seem to want.
Only you can wipe away from my eyes the blank stare of the breathing dead.
Only you can call me into aliveness.
Each time you're kind and gentle and encouraging, each time you try to
understand because you really care, my heart begins to grow wings,
very small wings, very feeble wings, but wings!
With your power to touch me into feeling you can breathe life into me.
I want you to know that.
I want you to know how important you are to me, how you can be a creator
—an honest-to-God creator — of the person that is me if you choose to.
You alone can break down the wall behind which I tremble,
you alone can remove my mask, you alone can release me front my shadow-
world of panic and uncertainty, from my lonely prison, if you choose to.
Please choose to. Do not pass me by. It will not be easy for you.
A long conviction of worthlessness builds strong walls.
The nearer you approach to me the blinder I may strike back.
It's irrational, but despite what the books say about man, often I am irrational.
I fight against the very thing that I cry out for.

But I am told that love is stronger than strong walls, and in this lies my hope.
Please try to beat down those walls with firm hands
but with gentle hands for a child is very sensitive.

Who am I, you may wonder? I am someone you know very well.
For I am every man you meet and I am everywoman you meet.

—Charles C. Finn

## 2     Patient Trust in the Slow Work of God

Above all, trust in the slow work of God.
We are quite naturally impatient in everything
to reach the end without delay.
We should like to skip the intermediate stages.
We are impatient of being on the way to something
unknown, something new.
And yet it is the law of all progress
that it is made by passing through
some stages of instability—
and that it may take a very long time.
And so I think it is with you;
your ideas mature gradually—let them grow,
let them shape themselves, without undue haste.
Don't try to force them on,
as though you could be today what time
(that is to say, grace and circumstances
acting on your own good will)
will make of you tomorrow.
Only God could say what this new spirit
gradually forming within you will be.
Give Our Lord the benefit of believing
that his hand is leading you,
and accept the anxiety of feeling yourself
in suspense and incomplete. — Pierre Teilhard de Chardin, SJ

# 3    Trauma Self-Assessments

I (CW) was a member of the CDC's *Adverse Childhood Experiences* study team from just before 1998 wherein we looked at how repeated trauma effected, produced, influenced or made the adult's life. We found that a questionnaire helped identify trauma survivors as adults (see below). We called these ACEs.

## 3 A.    ACE Study *Survey* –Adverse Childhood Experiences

*Prior to your 18th birthday: Please circle your honest answers*

1.    Did a parent or other adult in the household *often* . . .
       Swear at you, insult you, put you down, or humiliate you?

                                                *or*

       Act in a way that made you afraid you might be physically hurt?

                                                Yes    No

2.    Did a parent or other adult in the household *often* . . .
                      Push, grab, slap, or throw something at you?

                                                *or*

                      Ever hit you so hard that you had marks or were injured?

                                                Yes    No

3.    Did an adult or person at least five years older than you *ever* . . .
       Touch or fondle you or have you touch their body in a sexual way?

                                                *or*

       Attempt or actually have oral, anal, or vaginal intercourse with you?

                                                Yes    No

4.    Did you **often** feel that . . .
        No one in your family loved you or thought you were important or special?

                                                *or*

       Your family didn't look out for each other, feel close to each other, or support each other?

                                                Yes    No

5.    Did you **often** feel that . . .
       You didn't have enough to eat, had to wear dirty clothes, and had no one to protect you?

                                                *or*

       Your parents were too drunk or high to take care of you or take you to the doctor if you needed it?

                                                Yes    No

6.    Were your parents ever separated or divorced?

Yes    No

7.    Was your mother or stepmother . . .
      **Often** pushed, grabbed, slapped, or had something thrown at her?

*or*

**Sometimes** or **often** kicked, bitten, hit with a fist, or hit with something hard?

*or*

***Ever*** repeatedly hit for a few minutes or threatened with a gun or knife?

Yes    No

8.    Did you live with anyone who was a problem drinker or alcoholic or
      who used street drugs?          Yes    No

9.    Was a household member depressed or mentally ill, or did a
      household member attempt suicide?      Yes    No

10.   Did a household member go to prison?

Yes    No          From above, Number of Yes answers = _____

## B.      Interpreting My Answers to the *ACE Study* Survey

The *more Yes answers* to this survey are correlated and linked with the
person's later (after the traumas) having had more
• *chronic* and acute *medical problems,*
• *addictions,*
• *legal,*
• *social* and *relationship difficulties* and related
• **problems in living**.
For those people who had *four or more* adverse childhood experiences, the
following disease conditions and the risk factors for each were found to be
*substantially* more common when compared to those persons with no ACEs
(see table A.1 below).

## C.  Table A.1  Common *Long* Term Effects of ACEs (= *repeated trauma*)

| Infancy | Childhood | Teenage | Adulthood | Comments |
|---------|-----------|---------|-----------|----------|
| ← Increased *injuries* → | | ... Chronic illness begins | Chronic illness | ACEs likely most common cause of chronic plus mental illness |
| Delayed development | Behavior problems | Addictions - alcohol, drugs, tobacco, food, co-dependence, screens | | |
| | Low school grades | Emotional problems, suicide, un-wed pregnancy, abuse own children. Victimization | | Most are mis-diagnosed, PTSD underlies most |
| | | ↑ Risk taking | Cancer | |
| ... Disability can occur at any age | | | | |

- Adverse Childhood Experiences (ACEs) are very **common**, but *largely unrecognized*.
- **Strong predictors of later decreased social functioning, well-being, health risks, disease, medical costs, disability and death.**
- ACEs are thus the basis for much of adult medicine and of many major public health and social problems.
- ACEs are → **Not screened for** in *schools*, in nearly *all medical offices*, including *psychiatry*.
- The ACE study did **not** address Adverse **Adult** Experiences (AAEs), but the *Stressful Life Events* screen below does.

**D.  *To Heal*** — If you have had any of these life problems and you want to *explore how to heal* around these traumas with a safe and skilled person such as a counselor or therapist, we suggest that you find one that **specializes** in **trauma treatment**. Do *not* go to a general counselor or therapist or a physician, and especially not to a psychiatrist who trained after 1987 (the start of the Prozac era).

A good way to **find** a **trauma-skilled helper** is to go to an ACA (Adult Children of Alcoholics or Trauma meeting [Go online to → AdultChildren.org /meeting-search/]) and after the meeting ends ask a few attendees. You can also try a Co-dependence Anonymous (CoDA, coda.org/) meeting and do the same.

Author self-disclosure — We had several: BW had 7 ACEs, CW had 4 ACEs and each has had several *Stressful Life Events* (see below).

## E.  What are the traumas?
## Parental Conditions that Tend to Traumatize the Child/Teen/Young Adult

How can a mother, other parent figure or, later in life, a close friend be *able to help us meet* many of *our needs*? In general, to do so they must have had their needs met as children and/or worked through a process as adults of healing their own Child Within and learning to get their needs met.

However, certain conditions may interfere with getting needs met. The more deprived, more severe, or advanced the parent's and family's dysfunction or condition, the less the child's needs tend to be met. These parental conditions are listed in Table 3. The word "parental" means *not only the parent*, but may also include *siblings* and anyone else, and in the life of an older child and certainly in that of an adult refers to *any close* or *otherwise influential person*.

## F.
### Table A.7. The *Parents' Conditions*
### that Tend to *Traumatize* the Child and Later Adult

- **Alcoholism**
- **Other Chemical Dependence**
- **Co-Dependence (Neurosis)**
- **Chronic Mental Illness** and **Dysfunctional Physical Illness**
- **Extreme rigidity, punitive, judgmental, non-loving, perfectionistic, inadequacy**
- **Child abuse**—physical, sexual, mental-emotional, spiritual
- **Other conditions**, *e.g.*, those associated with post-traumatic stress disorder.

Any reader who wonders or is concerned about a parent's or another relative's drinking or drug use *or other behavior* may find it helpful to answer • the ACE study Screen and/or the simple questions in • the *Family Drinking Survey* (from page 26 in my book *Healing the Child Within*).

**4  The ACE Pyramid** represents the conceptual framework for the ACE Study, which has uncovered how *Adverse Childhood Experiences* (i.e., **repeated trauma**) are strongly related to various risk factors for disease throughout the lifespan. See page 151 in Chapter 14 on **Naming Traumas**.

*[handwritten: 149]*

**5  STRESSFUL LIFE EVENTS** SCREENING QUESTIONNAIRE - *REVISED*
The items listed below refer to events that may have taken place at any point in your life, including early childhood (Please print or write neatly)

1. Have you ever had a **life-threatening *illness*?**
No _____ Yes _____ If yes, at what age? _____ Duration of Illness _____
Describe specific illness _____

2. Were you ever in a **life-threatening *accident*?**
No _____ Yes _____ If yes, at what age? _____ Describe accident_____
Did anyone die? _____ Who? (Relationship to you)_____
What physical injuries did you receive? _____
Were you hospitalized overnight? No_____ Yes _____

3. Was **physical force** or a **weapon** ever used against you in a **robbery or mugging**?
No _____ Yes _____ If yes, at what age? _____
How many perpetrators?_____ Describe physical force (e.g., restrained, shoved) or weapon used against you. _____
Did anyone die? _____ Who? _____
What injuries did you receive? _____
Was your life in danger? _____

4. Has an immediate **family member, romantic partner**, or very **close friend *died*** because of **accident, homicide, or suicide**?
No _____ Yes _____ If yes, how old were you? _____How did this person die? _____Relationship to person lost _____
In the year before this person died, how often did you see/have contact? _____
Have you had a **miscarriage**? No _____ Yes _____ If yes, at what age?_____

5. At any time, has **anyone** (parent, other family member, romantic partner, stranger or someone else) ever physically **forced** you to have **intercourse**, or to have **oral or anal sex** against your wishes, or when you were helpless, such as being asleep or intoxicated? No _____ Yes _____ If yes, at what age? _____If yes, how many times?
If repeated, over what period? _____ Who did this? _____
Has *anyone else* ever done this to you? No_____ Yes _____Who? _____

6. Other than experiences mentioned in earlier questions, has anyone **ever touched private parts of your body, made you touch their body, or tried to make you to have sex against your wishes**? No _____ Yes _____ If yes, at what age? _____
If yes, how many times? _____ If repeated, over what period? _____ Who did this?
(Specify sibling, date, etc.) _____ What age was this person? _____

Has *anyone else* ever done this to you? No_____ Yes_____

7. When you were a child, did a parent, caregiver or other person ever **slap** you repeatedly, **beat** you, or otherwise **attack** or **harm** you? No _____ Yes_____ If yes, at what age _____ If yes, how many times? _____ Describe force used against you (e.g., fist, belt)_____ Were you ever injured? _____ If yes, describe _____ Who did this? _____

Has *anyone else* ever done this to you? No _____ Yes _____

8. **As an adult,** have you ever been **kicked, beaten, slapped around or otherwise physically harmed** by a romantic partner, date, family member, stranger, or someone else? No _____ Yes _____ If yes, at what age? _____If yes, how many times? _____ If repeated, over what period? _____Describe force used against you (e.g., fist, belt) _____Were you ever injured?_____ If yes, describe _____Who did this? (Relationship to you) _____ If sibling, what age ? _____Has *anyone else* ever done this to you? No_____ Yes _____

9. Has a parent, romantic partner, or **family** member **repeatedly ridiculed** you, **put you down, ignored you**, or told **you were no good**? No _____ Yes _____ If yes, at what age? _____ If yes, how many times? _____If repeated, over what period? _____Relationship to you) _____If sibling, what age? _____

Has anyone else ever done this to you? No_____ Yes _____

10. Other than the experiences already covered, has anyone ever **threatened you with a weapon like a knife or gun**? No ____ Yes _____At what age? _____ If yes, how many times? _____ If repeated, over what period? _____Nature of threat _____ Who did this? _____Has anyone else ever done this to you? No_____ Yes _____

11. Have you ever been **present when another person was killed**? **Seriously injured**? **Sexually or physically assaulted**? No _____ Yes _____If yes, at what age? _____ Please describe what you witnessed _____ Was your own life in danger? _____

12. Have you ever been in any **other situation where you were seriously injured** or your **life was in danger** (e.g., involved in military combat or living in a war zone)? No_____ Yes_____ If yes, at what age? _____ Please describe.

_____

13. Have you ever been in **any other situation** that was extremely frightening or horrifying, or one in which you felt extremely helpless, that you haven't reported? No_____ Yes_____ If yes, at what age? _____ Please describe. _____

# Interpreting My Answers to the STRESSFUL LIFE EVENTS
## Screening Questionnaire

Follow the same **Interpreting My Answers** to the *ACE Study* Survey about traumas.

# 6    **Near-Death Experience** of Barbara Harris Whitfield

### *No Wonder ~ No Wonder ~ No Wonder*

Even though I had been an atheist for years, I felt God's love. This love was holding me. It felt incredible. There are no words in the English language, or maybe in this reality, to explain the kind of love God emanates. God was totally accepting of everything we — God and I — reviewed in my life.

In every scene of my life review I could feel again what I had felt at various times in my life. And I could feel everything that everyone else had felt as a consequence of my presence and my actions. Some of it felt good and some of it felt awful. All of this translated into knowledge, and I learned. Oh, how I learned!

The information was flowing at an incredible speed that probably would have burned me up if it hadn't been for the extraordinary Energy holding me. The information came in, and then love neutralized my judgments against myself.

In other words, throughout every scene I viewed, information flowed through me about my perceptions and feelings, and the perceptions and feelings of every person who had shared those scenes with me. No matter how I judged myself in each interaction, being held by God was the bigger interaction. God interjected love into everything, every feeling, every bit of information about absolutely everything that went on, so that everything was all right. There was no good and no bad. There was only me -- and my loved ones from this life -- trying to survive... just trying to be.

I realize now that without God holding me, I would not have had the strength to experience what I did.

When it started, God and I were merging. We became one, so that I could see through God's eyes and feel through God's heart.

Together, we witnessed how severely I had treated myself because that was the behavior shown and taught to me as a child. I realized that the only big mistake I had made in my thirty-two years of life was that I had never learned to love myself.

God let me into God's experience of all this. I felt God's memories of these scenes through God's eyes. I could sense God's divine intelligence, and it was astonishing. God loves us and wants us to wake up to our real selves, to what is important. I realized that God wants us to know that we only experience real pain if we die without living first. And the way to live is to give love to ourselves and to others. It seems that we are here to learn to give and receive love. But only when we heal enough to be real can we understand and give and receive love the way love was meant to be.

When God holds us in our life reviews and we merge into One, we remember this feeling as being limitless. God is limitless. God's capacity to love is never-ending. God's love for us never changes, no matter how we are. God doesn't judge us either. During our life review, we judge ourselves by feeling the love we have created in other's lives. We also feel the pain we have caused in other's lives. This may be a kind of Cosmic Equalizer. I did not see an old man with a white beard who sits in judgment of us. I only felt limitless divine love.

God only gives. God interjected love into all the scenes of my life to show me God's reality. And the most amazing part of all is that God held nothing back.

I understood all that God understood. God let me in. God shared all of God's self with me: all the qualities of gentleness and openness, and all the gifts, including our own empowerment and peace. I never knew that much loving intelligence and freedom could exist.

At this point God and I were merging into one Sacred Person. It felt as though I lifted off the circle bed and We went to the baby I was seeing to my upper left in the darkness. Picture the baby being in a bubble; that bubble was in the center of a cloud of thousands and thousands of bubbles. In each bubble  was another scene from my life. As we moved toward the baby, it was as though we were bobbing through the bubbles. At the same time, there was a linear sequence in which we relived thirty-two years of my life. I could hear myself saying, 'No wonder, no wonder.' I now believe my 'no wonders' meant 'No wonder you are the way you are now. Look what was done to you when you were a little girl.'

My mother had been dependent on prescription drugs, angry and abusive, and my father wasn't home much of the time and did little to intervene. I saw all this again, but I did not see it in little bits and pieces, the way I had remembered it as an adult. I saw and experienced it just as I had lived it at the time it first happened. Not only was I me, I was also my mother, my dad,

and my brother. We were all one. Just as I had felt everything my grandmother had felt, I now felt my mother's pain and neglect from her childhood. She wasn't trying to be mean. She didn't know how to be loving or kind. She didn't know how to love. She didn't understand what life is really all about. And she was still angry from her own childhood, angry because they

were poor and because her father was sick almost every day until he died when she was eleven. And then she was angry because he had left her. She didn't know what to do with her anger so she gave it to my brother and me.

Her anger boiled up all the time and then she physically abused us or she made us listen to all her resentments. Her list went back to her early childhood. Everyone had hurt her. I don't think that she, through her numbness and drugged state, understood how she was doing the same thing to us.

Everything came flooding back, including my father's helplessness and confusion at stopping the insanity. I could hear myself saying, 'No wonder, no wonder.' And then the benevolent Energy that was holding me held me tighter and with even more love.

We continued watching my mother in pain, always seeing doctors and always receiving prescription painkillers, sleeping pills and tranquilizers. My only feeling during this time was loneliness. I saw myself down on my knees by the side of my bed, praying for a doctor to help my mother. I saw how I had given up 'myself' in order to survive. I forgot that I was a child. I became my mother's mother. I suddenly knew that my mother had had the same thing happen to her in her childhood. She took care of her father, and as a child she gave herself up to take care of him. As children, she and I both became anything and everything others needed.

As my life review continued, I also saw my mother's Soul, how painful her life was, how lost she was. And I saw my father and how he put blinders on himself to avoid his grief over my mother's pain and to survive. In my life review, I saw that they were good people caught in helplessness. I saw their beauty, their humanity and their needs that had gone unattended to in their own childhoods. I loved them and understood them. We may have been trapped, but we were still Souls connected in our dance of life by an Energy source that had created us.

This was when I first realized that we do not end at our skin. We are all in this big churning mass of consciousness. We are each a part of this consciousness we call God. And we are not just human. We are Spirit. We were Spirit before we came into this lifetime. We are all struggling Spirits now, trying to get 'being human' right. And when we leave here, we will be pure Spirit again.

As my life review continued, I got married and had my own children and saw that I was on the edge of repeating the cycle that I had experienced as a child. I was on prescription drugs. I was in the hospital. I was becoming like my mother. And at the same time, this Loving Energy we call God was holding me and let me into Its experience of all this. I felt God's memories of these scenes through God's eyes, just as I had through my grandmother's eyes.

As my life unfolded, I witnessed how severely I had treated myself because that was the behavior shown and taught to me as a child. I realized that the only big mistake I had made in my life was that I had never learned to love myself.

And then I was back here, in this reality. —> *Center*

# 7     History of Kundalini (by BW)

After centuries of hiding in nearly every culture on Earth under the guise of a secret esoteric truth, the Kundalini Awakening experience is increasingly reported among modern spiritual seekers. It appears to happen even among people who are not pursuing disciplined or esoteric spiritual practices. When this happens to those who have no understanding of the profound correlations between the physical and mystical experiences, it can leave them bewildered and frightened, even confused and dissociated. When they turn to traditional physicians, psychotherapists or church counsellors, their anxiety is often compounded by the general lack of understanding in Western culture regarding the potentiality in the human psyche for having profound spiritual emergence and its relationship to energy.[ii]

William James provided a description of the **mystical** experience, in his famous collection of lectures published in 1902 as *The Varieties of Religious Experience.* These criteria are

- **Passivity** - a feeling of being grasped and held by a superior power not under your own control.
- **Ineffability** - no adequate way to use human language to describe the experience.
- **Noetic** - universal truths revealed that are unable to be acquired anywhere else.
- **Transient** - the mystical experience is only a temporary experience.

From the research how this Energy manifests itself in NDE experiencers we named it as the physio-Kundalini syndrome.[iii] We used the Eastern Religion and medical model of Kundalini because it is mapped in a more sophisticated model than here in the West where we are just beginning to recognize energy medicine as an important part of our physical and mental health.

From 1990 on I (BW) have been a board member and on the board of the Kundalini Research Network. We bring in experts from all over the world to report their findings at our conferences. Bruce Greyson and I completed a scientific study of the physio-Kundalini hypothesis. He reported those results at the 1992 Kundalini Research Network Conference.

Some research details: As a group, Near-Death Experiencers reported experiencing almost twice as many physio-Kundalini items as did people who had close brushes with death but no NDE, as well as people who had never come close to death. Could the physio-Kundalini questionnaire be measuring non-specific strange experiences? To answer that possibility we added into the analysis the responses of a group of hospitalized psychiatric patients. They reported the same number of physio-Kundalini [index] items as did the non-NDE control group. There were two unexpected and ambiguous "control" groups in our studies: people who claimed to have had NDEs but described experiences with virtually no typical NDE features; and people who denied having had NDEs but then went on to describe prototypical near-death experiences. In their responses to the physio-Kundalini questionnaire, the group that made unsupported claims of NDEs were comparable to the non-NDE control group, while the group that denied having NDEs (but according to their responses on the NDE scale, did) were comparable to the group of NDErs. In regard to awakening Kundalini, then, having an experience mattered, but thinking you had one didn't.

**Manifestations** Because Western medicine does not yet acknowledge the East's physio-Kundalini model, symptoms of the arousal are often diagnosed as physical and/or psychological problems that fit within the Western allopathic diagnostic categories. For example, the physical shaking, twisting and vibrating so well known to experiencers could be diagnosed as a neurological disorder. It is hard to recognize the energy presence because it manifests itself in so many different patterns. Because its symptoms mimic so many disorders of the mind and body, even people familiar with the Energy concept are unsure whether they are witnessing rising Energy or distresses of the mind and body. The danger is in accepting prescriptions for drugs that Western physicians give to alleviate symptoms and possibly stopping the continuation of this natural healing mechanism. Any symptoms that can be alleviated by using this model should not usually be treated and suppressed with drugs.

In studying the manifestations that the Energy arousal may take, Greyson, Barbara Harris Whitfield and Ring compiled a questionnaire entitled *The Physio-Kundalini Syndrome Index*, containing 19 manifestations in three categories:

**Manifestations (i.e., Symptoms or Signs)**
**Motor or Movements**
- . Spontaneous body movements
- . Strange posturing
- . Breath changes
- . Body locking in certain positions

**Senses or Sensory**
- . Spontaneous tingling or vibrations
- . Orgasmic sensations
- . Progression of physical sensations up the legs and back and over the head
- . Extreme heat or cold sensations (in isolated areas of the body)
- . Pain that comes and goes abruptly

- •. Internal lights or colors that light up the body (or are seen internally)
- •. Internal voices (and internal whistling, hissing or roaring noises)

**Psychological**
- Sudden bliss or ecstasy for no reason
- Sudden anxiety or depression for no reason
- Speeding or slowing of thoughts
- Expanding beyond the body
- Watching the body from a distance

They surveyed 321 people (of which there were 153 NDErs, 55 who had come close to death but had no NDE, and 133 who never came close to death). These are *not small numbers*.

Among these i.e., NDErs had between 7 and 8 positives or 'yes' answers to the above symptoms or signs (see Kundalini Experiences questionnaire in section 13 below on page 220). These had about twice as many Kundalini symptoms or signs than among the 55 who had come close to death but had no NDE, and 133 who never came close to death [iv]

Ken Ring and Christopher Rosing reported almost identical results as ours in their research, *The Omega Project*: 'Near-death experiencers reported experiencing almost twice as many physio-Kundalini items as did people who had close brushes with death but no NDE, and people who had never come close to death.'

## The Concept of Energy
This Energy is a natural phenomenon with intense psychological and physical effects that can raise a person into a higher state of consciousness. This analysis is based on the reality that each of us has higher dimensions within our consciousness. As fields of consciousness, we have a spirit-body made of various energy systems. Various experiences can manifest in the Energy or spirit body. These can be highly emotional and are usually connected to activities in the autonomic nervous system and the hormonal and muscular systems of the physical body. These experiences can be repressed in our memories but are manifested as stress in our energy/spirit/biological body. Felt as "blocks in our energy," they can be released emotionally and physically.[v] Thus, Energy is fueled by emotion and can help us to release a lifetime of buried stress, resulting in our being a physically, emotionally, mentally and spiritually healthier person.

Whether this energy is called Chi, Ki, prana, Kundalini, bioenergy, Holy Spirit, vital force or simply Energy, we might consider adding the term 'Dragon Energy' to this list. The assumptions about it are similar. These include several healing aids using a concept of releasing this stored energy. These include Shiatsu, polarity, acupuncture, acupressure, Reikian body work, bioenergy integration, holotropic breathwork, T'ai Chi and some forms of massage.

In discussing an Energy model, there is a common limitation set up by the tendency to concretize the energy, to make it tangible, to view it as physical matter with physical properties. The concept of Energy in the human body, and any form of life, is best understood as dynamic, as a verb and not a noun. There is no such thing as Energy in physical form. Rather, there is activity described in energetic terms.

So when we speak of Energy, we characterize activity, not a measurable physical entity. According to the Chinese explanation, Energy is like the wind, invisible but with visible effects such as waves on a pond stirred by a breeze. The concept of Energy is a useful way of describing the deeper hidden patterns and processes that underlie the more visible effects. The results of the Energy, the visible waves on the pond, can be seen in the lives that we lead, the love that we share and the selfless service that we extend. Or as the New Testament puts it, "By their fruits you shall know them." (Matthew 7:20.)

This invisible Energy appears to be a deep, hidden pattern or process of integration that unifies all of our attributes, physical, mental, emotional and spiritual. We could also call it the creative intelligence that is working to make us whole.[vi] There are many different aspects to our Energy that manifest in different ways. Dragon Energy, as we describe through this book, is powerful if and when we identify, initiate and claim it.

## 8    Chakras - Energy Centers of Transformation

Everything in our known universe is *made up of* or *emits*, light and information, or *energy* and *consciousness*. That means your body is not only made up of these energies, but it is consistently and continuously sending and receiving light and information or energy and consciousness.

The energy centers in your body that we call *Chakras* are centers of information or *levels of consciousness*. Each center has a plexus of neurons that is correlated to a particular gland in your body.

**Chakra** is Sanskrit for *wheel* and describes energy centers or transducers that convey energy from one level into another. There are seven major chakras, and more minor ones, contained in our subtle energy body, that interact with our physical body. Each can be visualized as a center where many of the streams of energy -nadis or meridians- come together through the human body. *Each chakra* *mediates a different level of consciousness with the outer environment.*

This chakra system works for our growth and healing potential. Chakras modulate discrete frequencies that represent every variety of human experience on the mental, emotional, physical and spiritual levels. A pain in our hearts, a bright idea, a gut feeling, a tingling up our spines are a few examples of experiences originating in the vortex of a chakra energy center. So are experiences of oneness, sexual desire, self-pity, a beautiful singing voice and even addictions. [vii] A lump in our throat, butterflies in our stomach, pressure in our heads, all originate from a chakra picking up our inner life or perceiving the outer environment, then broadcasting it to us through our physical system until we feel it can focus us on to it.

## Associating our Levels of Consciousness with the Chakras helps us Understand Dragon Energy

After a spiritual awakening, it can feel so good that many of us want to stay in the higher levels of consciousness, higher chakras, higher spiritual levels and not deal with the lower three levels. However, we will have more Dragon Energy when we balance all seven, as summarized in Table A.2 below.

Table 8 A.2 **Levels of Consciousness, Chakras & Dragon Energy**

| Chakra/Level | Addresses | More | Dragon Energy |
|---|---|---|---|
| **7** - Crown | Spiritual | Indefinable | **God connection** |
| **6** - 3rd Eye | Perception | Flow, Love | **Observer Self** |
| **5** - Throat | Expression | Natural knowing | **Communication** |
| **4** - True Self, Heart | Lives as Real Self | Acceptance through conflict | **Strongest base level of functioning** |
| **3** - ego | Power | Primitive mental | **For survival only** |
| **2** - Sacral | Passion, Sex | Feelings, emotions | **Primitive emotions** |
| **1** – Root | Survival | Security, grounding | Use only ego |

→ Levels 1 through 3 represent **3 D**imensional consciousness and living.

→ Levels 4 and 5 represent **4 D** consciousness and living.

→ Levels 6 and 7 represent **5 D** consciousness and living.

Beginning at the bottom, the *first, root,* or **base chakra** is located at the base of the spine and opens down toward the ground. It keeps us alive in the body and draws sustenance from the Soul or True Self (see section 10 below). It is our sense of *grounding,* and ego *survival* and *security.*

Grounding requires the willingness, honesty and courage to face ourselves as we are and our world as it is – no denial, no exclusions, no avoidances, and no anesthesia. When we are solidly grounded our 4<sup>th</sup> Level heart chakra can function openly because our 1st chakra is balancing it.

The **second** *chakra* is said to be located about two inches below the navel and involves emotions and sex. When healthy and well-balanced, it is associated with being able to accept our own feelings and tolerate others'. Ideally, when we are balanced here we feel at peace. If hurt was done to us though this chakra from trauma or if it is out of balance now for some other reason, there is commonly a sense of separation, abandonment, rejection, anger, rage, fear of loss, etc. Many teachers believe that this is the chakra of emotional healing, going back to early childhood development.

The **third** *chakra* is called the solar plexus and is located at the level of the diaphragm. It is ego-based and we caution about it below on ego inflation. [ix]

Avoiding addressing these first three chakras can bring on a *spiritual bypass* or *high-level denial,* discussed below. Since we need to live in the physical world, we will achieve harmony and balance only by embracing these three levels of consciousness defined by the first 3 chakras.

During a **spiritual awakening**, our partially-dormant and often totally shut down upper four chakras may be aroused or opened. Anyone regularly pursuing psycho-spiritual growth will, over time, open these chakras. This may happen within the 4D Living Portal (pages 19 and 20). If we are aware of this and encourage these openings by doing our emotional work dealing with our unfinished business, we will know when our consciousness level is shifting from one level and chakra to another.

The **fourth** *chakra* is located at mid chest as our True Self (**Real Self**) or heart level. It is the **key** and **crucial hub** of our **mind** and relates to our capacity to use the intelligence, realness and creativity (page xxvi in *Introduction*). It also includes love and our ability to open our hearts and give. When this — our Real Self — level is blocked a person may appear to be cold or inhibited, or passive in their life.

This chakra also involves joyfulness and is the master control center for regulating the emotions. Many, if not most, NDErs that Bruce Greyson, Ken Ring and I interviewed appeared to have had a heart opening. You can tell by a vivid description of love — what we thought it was before and especially what we know it is now. In the classic *A Christmas Carol*, Scrooge's transformation at the end of the story is an excellent example of a heart chakra opening.

Occasionally some greedy relatives have taken NDE experiencers to court because of the after effects of a sudden heart opening where they want to give away their valuable possessions. Heart openings without healthy grounding can backfire and we can hurt ourselves, our families and unsuspecting others.

The **fifth** *chakra* is located in the throat and draws its abilities of expression as a synthesis of mind and heart energy from the Real Self 4$^{th}$ level. Those who have opened this center are able to *express* their heart experience of being alive. We are standing in the Light of our own soul. We are more in touch with ourself, others and the Universe.

The **sixth** *chakra* is between our eyebrows and often is called the 'third eye'. Its opening is often a result of regular spiritual practice, such as meditation and prayer. When this level opens there is a realization of unity, a blending of opposites, combining of male and female, mind and emotion, resistance and flow. Here we have the healthy dynamic of accepting and loving our self. [xi]

The **seventh** *chakra* at the top of the head funnels unlimited spiritual energy in and draws energy up from the lower centers in the process we know as enlightenment. We do not pray; we are prayer. We are no longer doing, just being. We have become our Higher Self connected to the God of our understanding. [x]

**A Word of Caution** This map of consciousness mediated through our Energy body has been studied in depth by ancient scholars and transpersonal scientists in the East and West. Yet there have been few descriptions to give Westerners a clear grasp of how this Energy and the chakra system can work in our lives when we are so embedded in Western culture. We found Lawrence Edwards' book *Awakening Kundalini* to be helpful.

At the same time, we can listen to our personal inner voice. As we travel our individual journeys, our mind's inner life will become clearer and that subtle voice stronger. Read and learn from all available teachers and guides, but keep only the knowledge and information that rings true for you. Beware of some rare or occasional teachers/gurus who may be out to exploit their students.

**Ego Inflation** (Negative Energy) The experiencers with painful symptoms who contacted Greyson and I were often scared, concerned, and wanted to know more. Some wanted to help with the research and occasionally claimed to be authorities. Some claimed that their Energy arousal had transformed them into gurus, which would suggest they have low humility.

Probably the biggest problem at this early stage of understanding is *ego inflation*. Many who have read the Eastern literature identify strongly with the gurus. Eventually we pass through this stage, realizing that we are Westerners and that it's hard to translate these Eastern metaphors when our cultural roots are so different. Our reward for getting through ego inflation is *humility*, which is the solid foundation of a truly spiritual, healthy and whole human being. Some don't experience ego inflation and others get stuck in it.

Humility is the willingness to continue learning our whole lives. Being humble is that state of being *open to learning about self, others and God*.[xi] A key way to getting Dragon Energy is to continually let go of our ego and live from and as our Real Self. In this focused awareness and practice we take responsibility to avoid ego attachment and can avoid the pitfalls of ego inflation and connect with God again here in this reality. In this state of humility and second innocence, we can experience whatever comes. [xii]

**Spiritual Bypass (Negative Energy)** Many of us know someone who has never done any inner work and is making everyone around them crazy with constant Bible or other source quoting or by extolling some definitive path. When I see someone pushing an exclusive, restrictive system, I become cautious. STEs are universal, *include everyone* and exclude no one. They include all beliefs, are *anti nothing*, *require no allegiance* and *embrace all*.

*References*
[i] Including physicians Evonne Kason, Bruce Greyson, Robert Turner and Lee Sannella.
[ii] From Energies of Transformation: A Guide to the Kundalini Process.
[iii] Bentov, Sannella, and Greyson 1992.
[iv] Ring and Rosing. "The Omega Project," The Journal of Near-Death Studies, 1990.
[v] Working with Kundalini energy and specifically by balancing the chakra system, alternative therapies suggested in this book can do more to alleviate these unwanted sensations than Western allopathic medicine has shown.

[vi] This information comes from an editorial I wrote for The Journal of Near-Death Studies (13:2, Winter 94) entitled "Kundalini and Healing in the West."

[vii] From a workshop and unpublished book by Gloria St. John, A Journey Throughout the Chakras. For further information see bibliography.

[viii] I caution against reading Kundalini literature during emotional turbulence because it can promote more energy flow, or awareness of energy flow into your body. Your ego/false self and True Self struggle for control, and focusing on Kundalini or Dragon Energy, or using it to distract can lead to ego inflation. Stay grounded. The waters are rough enough without making them rougher for yourself.

[ix] Whitfield B *Spiritual Awakenings: insights of the NDE and other doorways to our soul* 1995 HCI Deerfield Bch, FL

[x] Whitfield B op. cit.

[xi] Whitfield, Spirituality and Recovery, 1985.

[xii] Whitfield C & B, Parks R, Prevatt 2006 *The Power of Humility (HCI, Deerfield Beach, Florida)*

9

Update 7 all from sept vol 105 Ellen

## Table A.3  The 5 Dimensions to Raise Dragon Energy:

**Features & Characteristics** – *Continued as more information from* page 19 – 20.

| Dim. | Thinking | Choices | Balancing |
|---|---|---|---|
| 3 D | Linear, cause-and-effect, logical, reasonable, happen in steps, ego dominance common | Separation, Choices limited | Left brain, words & language, Reading & writing, Right brain less active |
| 4 D Port-al | Drop ego / Be Real / Name things accurately / Explore Inner Life Learn to love others and self. **Intention, desire** | The **portal** to increasing choices and balance | Letting go left brain, Right brain more active |
| 5 D | Multi-dimensional, Now | Choices unlimited | Balanced / words & language not primary |

From *The Ascension Council* (Six Members of the Council of Ascended Masters).

To receive monthly letters see *thecosmictimes.com*   UPDATE

**Dimension** – *convention*ally involves Length, Width, Height, Breadth, and Depth.

By contrast, 4 D involves the Portal process and 5 D is Multi-dimensional.

**Evolution of our Understandings of Dimensions over the Ages**

1) Anthropologists have shown you that in **pre-literate cultures that do not yet have an alphabet**, the world is perceived as wholeness, and events are **marked by song and poem**.

2) Only that which is already fully multi-dimensional will last: Fine art, music, literature, poetry, wisdom, numbers, love are all universal, and perfectly accessible in any dimension.

3) Reading and books are now taking a backseat to videos, emojis, comic books, and audios.

**5 D** - many of you (and especially your children) are taking in what you need to know much less through linear reading and more through the pictures of video, emojis, movies, comic books, texting, and audio-books. ...you are now "sliding into" 5D, you also can begin to hold a larger picture — so that, counter-intuitive though it may be, **you can grieve and rejoice at the same time**.

Linearity serves the Separation and limitation of 3D. Linear thinking means that you think in connected steps in a straight line, that one thing reasonably follows another, that things are logical and rational. If-then, or cause-and-effect, are linear.

## 10    Dragon Energy Helps Our Healing

While writing this book, I, Barbara took a hard fall and broke my leg. As I was lying on the cold floor waiting for an ambulance, I realized that everything in my peaceful and sometimes joyful life had just changed.

Having been in the health care field for over 40 years, I knew the threats that I now had to maneuver around including stroke and even death. An orthopedic surgeon met us in the emergency room and within a few hours corrected my fracture with two metal pins. Two days later I was transferred to an acute care rehab facility.

After years of treating patients after surgery, I expected a post-surgical depression to set in and part of me dreaded it. I had two good deep cries that lasted about 10 minutes each and I suspect there could be more. They feel like a great release valve if I don't try to control them by telling myself all kinds of ways to block or stop my acute grief. Sometimes, our bodies know better than our heads what is good for us.

Now here is the amazing surprise, the gift that has enveloped me. From the minute I opened my eyes after surgery and continuing two and a half weeks later in rehab, a profound natural gratitude has surfaced from deep within me. It wraps me in a deep resilience that shows up all the time and with humor too. I am shocked and delighted. This has nothing to do with positive thoughts. There is no "mind control" telling me how to behave.

Being deep into writing this book, Charlie and I realize this surprise gift is revitalizing my Dragon Energy. It knows better than my mind what is good for my healing. No one is more shocked than me by this wisdom. I could have never invented or created the way I am feeling.

Re-learning to walk, this morning while the physical therapist was pushing me to go beyond where I was yesterday and the days before that, I suddenly realized that my new 'mantra' is: 'I can!' And 'I can' is effortless because of Dragon Energy, which includes **being Real**, **grieving**, **being positive** and *making myself work* to strengthen my muscles as my leg heals.

A few years ago I co-authored a book we named AFGEs which stands for *Another F\*\*\*ing Growth Experience*.(Whitfield B, Cormier S, Muse House Press) I can reframe my broken leg as a growth experience which is also a synchronicity because it has shown me how DE works for me. When I *connect my DE to God through prayer* it gets even stronger.

I (CW) have been Barbara's caregiver throughout all this trauma recovery. She has had an amazing experience that I witnessed and experienced myself. We had 2 different roles in the same experience of unity with each other and God.

## 11 Kundalini Experiences questionnaire

*Please answer "Yes," "No," or "not sure" for each of the following questions:*

1. Does your body ever move spontaneously, without your wanting it to?

2. Does your body ever assume strange positions and hold them for some time?

3. Does your breathing spontaneously become very rapid, or shallow, or deep, or does it ever stop for an extended period?

4. Does your body ever become locked into a certain position, so that you cannot move it?

5. Does your skin or the inside of your body sometimes tingle, vibrate, itch, or tickle, for no apparent reason?

6. Do you ever have physical sensations of any type start in your feet, legs, or pelvis, and move up the back and neck to the top of the head, down the forehead, over the face, then to the throat, and end in the abdomen? (Answer "Yes" if you definitely have experienced <u>part</u> of this pattern.)

7. Do you ever feel a deep ecstatic tickle or a feeling like an orgasm for no apparent reason?

8. Do you ever have extreme feelings of heat or cold move through your body?

9. If so, have those extreme temperatures ever affected (i.e., burned) someone else or some object?

10. Have you ever "seen" internal lights or colors light up parts of your body?

11. If so, has that light ever been bright enough to enable you to see clearly in a darkened room?

12. Have you ever heard internal voices?

13. Have you heard other internal noises, such as whistling, hissing, chirping, roaring, or flute-like sounds?

14. Have you ever felt pains in specific parts of your body that began abruptly and then, after some time, ended abruptly, for no apparent reason?

15. Do you ever have sudden intense feelings of ecstasy, bliss, peace, love, devotion, joy, or cosmic harmony, for no apparent external reason?

16. Do you ever have sudden intense feelings of fear, anxiety, depression, hatred, or confusion, for no apparent external reason?

17. Do your thoughts ever speed up, slow down, or stop altogether?

18. Do you ever feel that you are watching all that is happening, including your own thoughts or feelings, from a distance – and while you are watching as if you are a detached bystander, your activities go on as usual?

19. Do you ever experience yourself to be physically larger than your actual body?

**Interpreting your score:** The Kundalini experience is not any form of a mental illness. It is a unique pattern of physiological and psychological effects. It is *not pathological*. But if you tell most any health professional that you may have any one of or a few of these signs or symptoms— from MDs to nurses to counselors — they will likely *not think of Kundalini* or a *spiritual awakening*.

*Bruce Greyson suggests that 'these data also bolster the claim that* **Kundalini is a natural process'** *(ibid. p. 54).* He also concludes that 'certain specific physio-kundalini symptoms can be identified as being particularly helpful in *differentiating kundalini awakening from mental illness' (ibid.* p. 56).
If you have 4 to 8 'yes' answers to the physio-kundalini symptoms above, we suggest that you would learn how to handle the signs and symptoms by
• Reading Barbara's book *Spiritual Awakenings*, see
• An expert acupuncturist who knows Kundalini,
• A Kundalini Yoga instructor, or an Ayurveda medicine practitioner, and
• Use regular prayer and meditation. Avoid general physicians, psychiatrists and most nurses *for these symptoms*. Avoid taking psychiatric drugs.

If you identify strongly with this list, and it feels like it is happening too fast, eat root veggies like carrots, potatoes etc. If you are vegetarian, eating a bit of red meat will help too. Greyson and I chaired an IANDS conference many years ago called 'Clinical Approaches to the Near-Death Experiences.' 32 therapists and medical doctors who were familiar with spiritual psychology came and for four days we went over signs, symptoms and approaches that would help people going through this process.

After the conference, a group of us who didn't have to leave immediately, walked to our closest McDonalds and ate their

French Fries. It seems the grease and root potato brought us 'down' before we had to

leave to travel to our homes all over the States, Europe and Australia. Four days of non-stop talking about spiritual symptoms and we knew we needed to get 'grounded.' There are times in this natural process where we can feel manic and need grounding.

A short time later we joined another research group called 'The Kundalini Research Network' (KRN) and for the next 20 years we met almost yearly to share what more we had discovered in the research. Again, researchers and clinicians from all over the globe came to discuss this natural phenomenon. Most if not all of us were functioning well in this process. The main sign in that we or our patients are doing well is *Humility* (for more on this see our book *The Power of Humility.)* Without humility there is ego inflation which not only can destroy the process from eventually completing, but can destroy relationships and finances. This can manifest in the person thinking they are now a guru and try to gather followers. Any teacher or guru who is looking for followers that don't show humility are not authentic. In my book *Spiritual Awakenings* I cover this in much greater depth. If and when this process begins we have heard and seen this manic reaction turn into what we named 'Spiritual Bypass.' Setting up an 'Ashram' a few days, weeks or months after a Kundalini 'arousal' without dealing with past traumas first is dangerous. The Kundalini process can take a lifetime to complete or even several lifetimes.

## 12    Origin of **Art of the Veils**

***Quests for knowledge***: On the next page we show the art of an unknown artist that has inspired many seekers of the truth. When we saw it last year after Dragon Con 2018 it stimulated our creative imaginations. Compare and discuss on it to Ciruelo's *perfect* drawing for our book about healthy Dragon Energy in our Special Section early on.

We were inspired last year when we saw this **Classic artwork** — not drawn or engraved — but *presented by* the astronomer and author Nicolas Camille Flammarion engraving by an *unknown artist* that dates back to 1888 in the book, 'L'atmosphère: météorologie populaire' (French for *The atmosphere: popular Meteorology*. After studying and contemplating it we conceived an expanded version which Ciruelo drew so well. (Flammarion lived for 83 years [a longer than usual life for his time] from 1842 to 1925.)

The image shows a man crawling under the edge of the sky, as if it were a solid hemisphere, to look at the mysterious Empyrean beyond (a word for 'the highest Heaven' from the Greek and used later in Dante's *Divine Comedy*).

The original caption translates to 'A medieval missionary tells that he has found the point where heaven and Earth meet...'

It has been used to represent a supposedly medieval cosmology, including a flat earth bounded by a solid and opaque sky, or firmament, and also as a ***metaphorical illustration*** of either the **scientific** and/or the ***mystical quests for knowledge***.

# REFERENCES

Adams D 1982: *Life, the Universe and Everything.* Harmony Books, NY

Anonymous 1976: *A Course in Miracles.* Foundation for Inner Peace, NY

Baggott J 2015: *Origins*: The Scientific Story of Creation. Oxford University Press

Bancroft A 1979: *Zen*: Direct Pointing to Reality. Crossroad NY

Breggin PR 2008: *Brain-Disabling Treatments in Psychiatry:* Drugs, electroshock, and the psychopharmacutical complex. 2nd edition Springer Publishing, NY.

Campbell J 1959: *The Historical Development of Mythology.* Originally in journal *Daedalus*, also in *The Mythic Dimension: Selected Essays 1959*

Campbell J 1991: *The Power of Myth.* Anchor

Campbell J 2008: *The Hero with a Thousand Faces* (The Collected Works of J Campbell). New World Library

Cavalli TF 2010: Embodying Osiris: The Secrets of Alchemical Transformation. Quest Books

Chambers J 2018: *The Metaphysical World of Isaac Newton*: Alchemy, Prophecy, and the Search for Lost Knowledge. Destiny Books

Cheny M 2011: *Nicola Tesla*: The extraordinary life of a modern Prometheus: The Entire Life Story. Touchstone

Christensen D, Tang Y 2004: *Christ the Eternal Tao.* St Herman Press

Coleman SL, Beitman BD, Celebi E 2009: Weird Coincidences commonly occur. *Psychiatr Ann* 39(5):265-270

Coston TO 1970: The proper symbol of medicine. *Trans Am Ophthalmol Soc* ;68:359–63

Cousineau (Editor), Brown SL, Campbell J 2014: *The Hero's Journey*: Joseph Campbell on His Life and Work. New World Library

Goddard D 1999: *The Tower of Alchemy*: An Advanced Guide to the Great Work. Red Wheel /Weiser

Goodrick-Clarke N 2008: *The Western Esoteric Traditions*: A Historical Introduction. Oxford University Press

Edwards L 1996: *The Soul's Journey*: Guidance from the Goddess Within. Self Published

Edwards L 2013: *Awakening Kundalini*: The Path to Radical Freedom. Sounds True, Boulder, Co

Friedlander WJ 1992: *The Golden Wand of Medicine:* A History of the Caduceus Symbol in Medicine. Greenwood Press NY

Greyson B and Harris (Whitfield) B 1987: Clinical Approaches to the NDE. *J Near-Death Studies* 6, (fall 87) 41-50

Greyson, CB 1992/98: A scientific study of the physio-Kundalini hypothesis. *Kundalini Research Network Conference*, Simpsonwood Conf Center, Peachtree Corners, Ga

Greyson, CB 2000: A scientific study of the physio-Kundalini hypothesis. *Journal of Transpersonal Psychology* 32:2

Grof S, Grof C Eds 1989: *Spiritual Emergency:* When personal transformation becomes a crisis. Los Angeles: Tarcher

Grof S 2019: *The Way of the Psychonaut.* Encyclopedia for Inner Journeys. vols One and Two, MAPS

Hanegraaf WJ, Faivre A, van den Broek R, Brach J 2006: *Dictionary of Gnosis & Western Esotericism*. Brill Boston

Hartle JB, Hawking SW 1983: Wave function of the universe. *Phys Rev* D 28, 2960 ; 1987: Adv Ser Astrophys Cosmol. 3, 174

Hawkins D 1958: *Power Vs. Force***:** The Hidden Determinants of Human Behavior. Hay House UK

Harari YN 2014: *Sapiens*: A Brief History of Humankind. Vintage

Hebrew Bible (*Old Testament).* Numbers 21:5-9 King James Translation.

Hillman J 1989: *A Blue Fire*: Selected writings by James Hillman. Harper & Row, NY

Hillman J 2017: *The Alchemy of Psychology.* Better Listen (Audiobook)

Hoffman E 1989: *The Right to be Human*: A Biography of *Abraham Maslow.* Tarcher

James W 1902: *The Varieties of Religious Experience* : A study in human nature. NY, Longmans, Green and Co

Johari H 1987: *Chakras*: Energy Centers of Transformation. Destiny Books, VT

Jourard SM 1964: *The Transparent Self.* Van Nostrand ... a classic on *Being Real*

Keim W 2009: *The Tao of Christ*: The way of love for a world of hurt. WillKeim.com

Kelly EF , Kelly EW, Grosso M, Crabtree A, Gauld A, Greyson B  2007: *Irreducible Mind*:⫯⫯
Toward a Psychology for the 21st Century. Roman & Littlefield

Khalsa GK, Wilber K, Krishna G, Walters D et al 2009: *Kundalini Rising*: Exploring the
Energy of Awakening. Sounds True, Boulder

Korzybski  A 1973: *Science and Sanity* : An Introduction to Non-Aristotelian Systems and
General Semantics.  Institute of General Semantics, Chicago

Lao Tsu 2016: *Tao Te Ching.*  Create Space Publishing , Amazon

Lehner E & J 1969/2004: *Big Book of Dragons, Monsters and Other Mythical Creatures.*
Dover Publications Mineola NY

Le Guin UK 2019: *Lao Tzu: Tao Te Ching*: A Book about the Way and the Power of the
Way . Shambhala, Boulder

Maslow A H 1971: *The Farther Reaches of Human Nature.* NY McGraw-Hill

Maslow A H 1968: *Toward a Psychology of Being.* 2nd ed Van Nostrand

Ming-Dao Deng 1992:  *365 TAO Daily Meditations.* Harper & Row

Mishlove J 1993: *The Roots of Consciousness*: The Classic Encyclopedia of Consciousness
Studies. Revised and Expanded. →Watch his excellent *Thinking Allowed* series online

Needleman J ed. 1974/1985: *The Sword of Gnosis*: Metaphysics, Cosmology, Tradition,
Symbolism.  Arkana Penguin

Nisbett RE, Peng K, Choi I, Norenzayan A 2001/4: Culture and systems of thought:
holistic versus analytic cognition. *Psychological review* 108:2, 291

Nisbett R 2004: *The Geography of Thought*: How Asians and Westerners think
differently... and why. NY Simon & Schuster

Osbon DK 1991  *Reflections on the Art of Living*: A Joseph Campbell Companion
Harper Perennial

Pagels E 1979: *The Gnostic Gospels.* NY Random House . A clear classic

Pagels E 1988: *Adam, Eve and the Serpent.* NY Random House

Patrick S 2013: *Nikola Tesla*: Imagination and the Man That Invented the 20th Century. Oculus Publishers

Perry R 2009: *Signs*: A New Approach to Coincidence, Synchronicity, Guidance, Life Purpose, and God's Plan. Sedona, AZ: Semeion Press

Peat FD 1987: *Synchronicity*: The Bridge Between Matter and Mind. Bantam, NY

Prakash M, Johnny JC 2015: Things you don't learn in medical school: Caduceus. *J Pharm Bioallied Sci.* 7 (Suppl 1): S49–S50

Ram Dass (Richard Alpert) 1974: *The Only Dance There Is*. Doubleday Anchor

Ram Dass (Richard Alpert) 1976: *The Only Dance There Is*. Unity Press, Santa Cruz

Ram Dass (Richard Alpert) 1978: *Be Here Now*. Harmony Books

Reidy K 2019: Here Be Dragons. Scientific American online article at blogs.scientificamerican.com/observations/here-be-dragons/

Richo D 2008 *The Power of Coincidence*: How Life Shows Us What We Need to Know. Shambhala

Ring K 1985: *Heading Toward Omega* : In Search of the Meaning of the Near-Death Experience. NY Morrow

Ring K 1992: *The Omega Project* : Near-Death Experiences, UFO Encounters and Mind at Large. NY Morrow

Ring K 2006: *Lessons from the Light*: What We Can Learn from the Near-Death Experience. Moment Point Press

Roob A 2001: *Alchemy & Mysticism*. Taschen, Hamburg

Sannella L 1977: *Kundalini, Psychosis or Transcendence?* HS Daikin San Francisco

Sanella L, White J, Bentov I 1990: Spiritually *Transformative Experience (STE)*. They helped Greyson, Ring and I to expand into the term *Physio-Kundalini Syndrome*

Schmidt D 2012: *Inner Worlds, Outer Worlds*. Documentary, Canada. Superb.

Shen T 2017 Recognition of symbols in different cultures: Chinese culture vs. non-Chinese culture. *Graduate Theses and Dissertations.* @ lib.dr.iastate.edu/etd/15420

Straiton V 2010:*The Celestial Ship of the North*. Kessinger Publishing

Sunfellow D 2019: *The Purpose of Life*: As revealed in near-death experiences from around the world. Bookdesigntemplates.com

Tansley DV 1977: *Subtle Body*: Essence and Shadow. Thames and Hudson

Wallas G, Smith R 1926: *Art of Thought*. Republished 2014 showing creativity in 4 Stages. Solis Press, UK

White J Ed 1990: *Kundalini*: Evolution and Enlightenment. Revised ed, Paragon House

Whitfield CL 2010: *Choosing God*: A Bird's-Eye-View of *A Course in Miracles.* Muse House Press

Whitfield CL 2014: *Teachers of God*: Further Reflections on *A Course in Miracles.* Muse House Press

Whitfield CL 1987: *Healing the Child Within*: Discovery and Recovery for Adult Children of Dysfunctional Families. Health Communications, Deerfield Beach, FL

Whitfield CL 1993, 2010: *Boundaries and Relationships*: Knowing, Protecting and Enjoying the Self. Health Communications, Deerfield Beach, FL

Whitfield CL, Silberg J, Fink P (eds): *Misinformation Concerning Child Sexual Abuse and Adult Survivors.* Haworth Press N.Y. 2002

Whitfield CL 1995: *Memory and Abuse*: Remembering and Healing the Effects of Trauma. Health Communications, Deerfield Beach, FL,

Whitfield CL 1998: Adverse Childhood Experiences and Trauma (editorial) *American Journal of Preventive Medicine* 14:361–363

Whitfield CL 2003: *The Truth about Depression*: Choices for Healing. Health Communications, Deerfield Beach, FL

Whitfield CL 2004: *The Truth about Mental Illness: Choices for healing.* Health Communications, Deerfield Beach, FL

Whitfield CL 2004: *My Recovery*: A personal plan for healing. Health Communications, Deerfield Beach, FL.

Whitfield CL, Whitfield BH, Prevatt J, Park R: *The Power of Humility*: Choosing Peace over Conflict in Relationships. Health Communications, Deerfield Beach, FL, 2006

Whitfield CL 2009: Spiritual Energy: Perspectives from the Map of the Psyche and the Kundalini Recovery process. *in* Khalsa GK et al 2009: *Kundalini Rising*: Exploring the Energy of Awakening. Sounds True, Boulder

Whitfield CL 2011: *Not Crazy*: You May NOT Be Mentally Ill. Muse House Press, Atlanta

Whitfield CL 2012: *Wisdom to Know the Difference*: Core Issues in Relationships, Recovery and Living. Muse House Press, Atlanta ... May be my *best book ever*

Whitfield CL 2010: Psychiatric drugs as agents of trauma. *Int J of Risk and Safety in Medicine* 22 (4)195-207

Whitfield CL, Whitfield BH 2013: *Timeless Troubadours*: The Moody Blues Music and Message. *Foreword* by MB's co-founder, keyboardist, composer and vocalist Mike Pinder. Muse House Press, Atlanta

Whitfield B 1995: *Spiritual Awakenings*: Insights of the Near-Death Experience and Other Doorways to our Soul. Deerfield Beach, Florida. Health Communications

Whitfield BH, Greenwell B, Luchakova O 1998: Understanding Kundalini: Quantum Evolution for the New Millennium, *Proceedings of the 7th International Symposium of the Kundalini Research Network Conference*, Simpsonwood Conference Center, Peachtree Corners/Norcross, Ga

Whitfield B 2010: *The Natural Soul*: Unity with the Spiritual Energy that Connects Us Muse House Press, Atlanta

Whitfield B and Cormier S 2015: *AFGEs: A Guide to Self Awareness and Change.* (AFGE = Another F***ing Growth Experience Muse House Press, Atlanta

Whitfield B 1990: *Full Circle-The Near Death Experience and Beyond.* Simon & Schuster

Whitfield B 2009: Mental and Emotional Health in the Kundalini Process. *in* Khalsa GK et al 2009: *Kundalini Rising*: Exploring the Energy of Awakening. Sounds True, Boulder

Whitfield B 2011: *Victim to Survivor and Thriver*: Hope for Survivors of Childhood Trauma, Abuse or Neglect Muse House Press Atlanta

Whitfield B 2015: *The Secrets of Medicinal Marijuana.* Muse House Press Atlanta Ga

Wilcox RA, Whitham EM 2003: The Symbol of Modern Medicine: Why One Snake Is More Than Two. *Annals of Internal Medicine*

END of REFs

# INDEX

## U
unconscious mind   95, 134, 188, 198

## V
vibrations   132-3, 211
victim   iii, ix, 65, 67, 175, 182-4, 231

## W
Western Dragons   38-9, 95
Westerners   72, 102, 216-17, 228
wings   41, 85, 95, 189, 200
wisdom   iii, xi-xiii, xv, xxx, 10, 31-2, 41-2,
49, 59-61, 73, 95, 159, 161, 163-4, 219

## Y
Yang   42, 72-4, 98-9
Yin   72-4, 98-9
Yin Yang   60, 73-4, 76, 86
yoga   xx, 54, 96-7, 100, 102, 106, 121, 133, 188, 194, 197

[Created with **TExtract** / www.Texyz.com]